# FARM

**A PORTRAIT OF PEOPLE, PLACES, AND IDEAS FOR A NEW FOOD MOVEMENT**

# TOGETHER

# NOW

**AMY FRANCESCHINI**

**DANIEL TUCKER**

PHOTOGRAPHS BY
**ANNE HAMERSKY**

FOREWORD BY
**MARK BITTMAN**

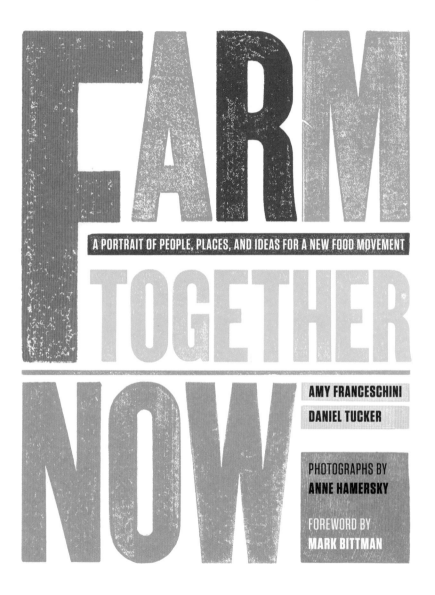

CHRONICLE BOOKS
SAN FRANCISCO

Library of Congress Cataloging-in-Publication Data available.

ISBN 978-0-8118-6711-5

Manufactured in China

Design by Brian Scott
Illustrations by Corinne Matesich
Transcription: Carla Avitabile, Alex Harker, Corrine Matesich,
Ashley Weger

10 9 8 7 6 5 4 3 2 1

Chronicle Books LLC
680 Second Street
San Francisco, California 94107
www.chroniclebooks.com

**Amy Franceschini:**
To my mother and father
for allowing me to see
the many paths in the fork.


**Daniel Tucker:**
To my parents for living
right and making time for
everything that matters.

# Contents

# Foreword: Farms Matter

## Mark Bittman

There has been a progression in the rediscovery of good food in the United States. In this process, which has taken place over the last fifty years, we first began to understand and appreciate that it was possible for home cooks to reproduce wonderful and classic food, primarily, but not exclusively, food based on French and American traditions. Soon thereafter, we recognized that restaurants could become temples of good cooking from all over the world.

But it wasn't long before we realized—we're talking late '70s, early '80s here—that the best cooking had a foundation that had been almost forgotten: good ingredients. Thus followed, in typical American fashion, an obsession with the "best" ingredients, which sometimes meant the most coddled (think of early heirloom tomatoes) and sometimes meant the most expensive (think truffles).

We have matured, or at least, we are maturing. We have worked our way through and even worshipped natural, organic, and local ingredients—as well as celebrity chefs and ultramodern cuisine—and we have come to understand that there are no panaceas. But along the way we have also come to see this always-obvious but sometimes overlooked fact: There is a fundamental process in producing fundamentally good ingredients—those raised, to use a clichéd but appropriate phrase, in harmony with nature.

That process, of course, is farming. But producing real ingredients takes a special kind of farming, and the farming that dominated the landscape by the '1960s—and which has for the most part grown worse with each passing decade—has raped the land, tortured animals, exploited workers, and disregarded the needs of consumers, all the while producing inferior food.

We need to do exactly the opposite, and part of the way the American food landscape has changed, and the greatest hope for its future, is the dedication of new farmers who've recognized that, committed to it, and become the new pioneers. These are the farmers who speak here.

Farming has always been work—hard work, in fact. But though mechanization has made the physical aspects of farming easier, the loss of traditional methods has in some ways made things more challenging. The modern, so-called efficient way to do things—industrially—is obviously unsustainable; we need another way.

The chances are good that if you're reading these words you know that already. You probably also know that a small but increasing number of farmers, represented in this book, are combining traditional ways with contemporary knowledge to search for and come up with a series of new systems that produce good food while treating the environment, animals, workers, and consumers with respect. Doing this while still making a living, in fact having a good life, is the great agricultural challenge facing the world in the twenty-first century.

There are no easy answers. It's one thing to restructure a farm and make things work in a relatively populated portion of the Midwest, such as Minneapolis or Kansas City; there is infrastructure and a nearby market, and a more traditional ratio of farmers to urban citizens. It's an entirely different thing to try to address the needs of a nation where four out of five of us live in cities. Unlike Kansas City (population 150,000), for example, New York (population 8,000,000) is not surrounded by farmland and farmers.

How, then, might we feed ourselves sustainably? That's the question that's addressed in these twenty essay-interviews, and the answers are almost as varied as the work that these farmers are doing.

What I hear, though, is a general agreement (and a sentiment I share) that we all need to be more involved in farming. Most of us are consumers, of course, and we'll remain so. But it's likely that more and more of us will become farmers, for a variety of reasons. There'll be fewer industrial jobs; we see this already. Food will inevitably rise in price, not only because it's more expensive to produce good food than mass-processed foodstuff, but also because resources are going to become scarcer and this, combined with declining land costs, will make it more attractive for young people to stay on family farms or start their own.

And even the vast majority of us who remain non-farmers will know and understand farming in a better way than older generations have: farms will necessarily come closer to cities (some will be *in* cities, which remains common in other countries), there will be more of them, and, as farmers' markets increase in number, we'll all be dealing more directly with the people who grow or raise our food.

I can't think of a better next step. With more farmers and better interaction between consumers and growers, we can continue to work on and eventually work out the answers to the big question: How do we feed ourselves not only well but sustainably?

# Introduction

During the summer of 2009, we visited the twenty farms featured in this book. Individually, each reveals some of the most exciting currents and possibilities for how we could perceive and receive the food we eat at this specific time in history. Collectively, they form a portrait of the complexity of farming in the United States today. We spent time with the individuals who grow food, in the places where they work—the environments that shape their crops and lives—and through these interviews, we hope to depict a sense of place, people, and action to challenge and inspire you.

We traveled from the shores of the Pacific Coast of California bordering Silicon Valley to the post-industrial landscapes of Holyoke, Massachusetts. The disparity of each farm amplified when we physically visited each location: the arid terrain of the Southwest in Patagonia, Arizona, compared to the gridded agricultural landscape surrounding California's San Joaquin Valley; urban gardens and farms in sprawling metropolises like Atlanta, Georgia, to rural farms on rolling hills like those found in Kendall, Wisconsin. Topping it off, the impressive agricultural cultures we encountered in the Rocky Mountains of Colorado and the Appalachian Mountains of North Carolina reminded us of challenging microclimates that people have been carefully adapting to for thousands of years.

In traveling across the United States, we found great inspiration from the struggles against corporate agriculture and the dramatic turns toward different food systems taking place. We stated from the start, when emailing farmers and organizations across the country, that "We want the way the food system works to change! So we chose to seek out and meet with people across the country who are doing just that!"

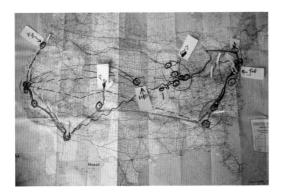

The twenty projects presented in this book profile various approaches. They reflect different and sometimes opposing philosophies. Many place themselves within subcultures currently working under banners such as "**food justice**," "sustainable agriculture," and "local-foods movement" and share their philosophies through education and demonstration. For some, it's through direct action or policy battles, and for others, their physical work and very local distribution is quite enough.

We chose to use the interview format as a way to bring the voices of the farmers and activists to you as directly as possible. While each profile can stand on its own, this collection is an exhibit of the people and places that are bound together by a common interest in food and its link to every aspect of life.

For each farm, we cover essential details: scale, working habits, influences, and organizational structure. We discuss philosophies, public policy, history, soil, and distribution methods. By understanding how these individuals are creating solutions for their lives and the lives of those whom they care about, we feel more optimistic about our future. We present their stories here because we know that a new food system can only emerge if the diversity and complexity that these folks embody are part of the discussion.

Definitions for terms in **bold type** can be found in the glossary starting on page 184.

We hope that you are as inspired by the individuals who have shared their voices as we are. Let's hear from them, learn from them, celebrate them, and join them. Let's farm together now!

# Knopik Family Farm

Location:
**Fullerton, Nebraska**

Organizing body:
**2, plus many more through various organizations**

Scale:
**1,000 acres for mob grazing, 400 for crops**

Type:
**For profit**

Currently producing:
**200 cows**

In operation:
**Since the late 1960s**

Web sites:
**North Star Neighbors: nebraskafood.org/ shop/producers/nstar.php**

**Nebraska Food Cooperative: nebraskafood.org**

Third-generation farmer Jim Knopik decided to protest when he found out that some very large "factory farm" meat producers were going to be moving to town and disrupting the local economy, and bringing along their environmentally toxic approaches to food production. In the process of mounting a resistance against the confined-animal feeding operation (**CAFO**), Knopik realized that his own farm was involved in some practices that were also ecologically unsustainable and were harming the animals and the land.

Knopik reformed his farming and founded North Star Neighbors with his wife, Carolyn, and a network of four farms in the region. North Star Neighbors is a direct-marketing cooperative specializing in raising beef, pork, lamb, chicken, turkey, and duck. Their Web site states: "Our animals are raised from birth on our farms. We know exactly what they eat from birth. They are never given antibiotics or artificial growth stimulants. No animal by-products are fed to our animals. Our animals are not grown in confinement buildings. They are raised on grass and in open lots and grain-finished on non-**GMO** (genetically modified organism) corn, soybeans, oats, and alfalfa. Our animals are taken directly from our farms to a family owned, **USDA**-inspected processing plant."

Recently elected county supervisor, Knopik is devoted to environmental activism and has started the statewide Nebraska Food Cooperative, which helps sustainable producers directly market their food online.

# Interview with Jim Knopik

**Could you talk about where you're from—the region, the people, your land?**
**Jim Knopik, owner**: I live ten miles west of Fullerton, Nebraska, in Nance County, which has a lot of different kinds of soil. I've lived on this farm since I was a year old. And now I'm sixty. When my dad started farming, it was all about sustainable agriculture. He would just get whatever the soil would give him. If he wanted fertilization, he did it through rotation. When I started, in the late '60s, we wanted to get bigger and be more productive—we started using synthetic fertilizers and chemicals in our farming operations.

**What was it that you saw on other people's farms that convinced you to make that switch?**
Less weeds in the field, for one thing—that's something farmers always like to have, clean fields. So if the chemicals can do that, you naturally move that way. It's a lot about image, too. If things don't look good, people won't listen to you. Image is everything.

**How has your livestock operation changed throughout the years?**
I raised hogs out in the open up until about ten years ago; we probably raised eighty to a hundred at a time. When I first started raising hogs, I could make fifteen dollars a head. If you sell a hundred of them, that's fifteen hundred dollars— a lot of money back in 1970. And then, around 1980, I built a confinement operation, which handled about five hundred at a time. But I found out that in confinement, animals' health becomes an issue. It got to bother me that I had to run around with a syringe in my pocket all the time, vaccinating hogs. When it came time to have those animals on medication twenty-four hours a day to keep them somewhat healthy, that's when, in my mind, it wasn't sustainable. I didn't think I was qualified to administer medicine in the way it needed to be done. But there was this "get big or get out" idea.

As time went on, and those profit margins went down to two or three bucks, well, you had to raise five times as many hogs to make the same amount of money. The [consolidation] of the industry just kept taking those margins away from the producers and putting them in the pockets [of big operations]. That's why now you see the big operations doing fifty thousand hogs.

Above:
Jim Knopik and grandson
Lane move the electric fence
and their herd twice a day.

**When did the CAFO factory farm try to move into your community?**
I think it was June 1997. That situation caused me to take a hard look at what we were doing on the farm. The way we operated then was by observing our responsibility as farmers to feed people. You hear on the radio that every farmer feeds 128 people—that's the kind of thing that keeps you in the seat for eighteen hours a day. That was propaganda, I think, but it made me work hard just the same. My responsibility was to society, to feed people.

But after the big hog guys came in and tried to push all of their hogs onto a small, little area in our community, I realized that I had isolated myself from what was really going on in the world. Once I saw what the **CAFO** was doing, I understood that I had to become more involved in my community. This was another kind of responsibility that wasn't just about working and keeping your nose to the grindstone.

So what happened was that, in June 1997, a real estate guy came in from out of town wanting to acquire some land that we rented. He wanted to meet me out on a dirt road near where the hog guys wanted to set up their hog site. And they wanted fifteen sites. There was something real fishy about the situation. This caused me to ask a lot of questions.

With a hog farm of my own, I knew some of the environmental impact that I was causing, but I was containing it on my property. Yet here they wanted to bring in half a million hogs into too small of an area. I could see what was going to happen.

Two weeks before I was approached, the mayor of Fullerton called me up and she asked me if [there were any] hog barns available. "What the hell is going on here?" I thought. "Why is everyone trying to do this undercover and not being really open about it?" I could see something wasn't right.

When I started asking questions, and once it finally broke open that the hog guys were going to come in here and [set up a **CAFO**], that's when people looked to me. In a matter of about four days, we went from 6 or 7 neighbors discussing it at coffee on Thursday morning to having more than 150 people at a meeting on Sunday night.

We grew that fast, and that night I was elected president of the organization! The organization was called Mid-Nebraska PRIDE (People Responding in Defense of our Environment).

**It seems like that is a big shift to happen so quickly.**
Oh, yeah. That was when I really transitioned from a farmer to an activist, I guess. I almost abandoned the farm because so many people were calling who were having the same problem across the state. You see, this hog guy was moving to other areas. Once those people found out about how we stopped him, through getting our community organized, we were called into their communities. We were doing town hall meetings, hell, probably twice a week during the next six months. And then, of course, we were having our internal meetings, oh, I would say, dang near every day—and sometimes twice a day. I figure we had 180 meetings the first year.

**How did North Star Neighbors grow out of your experience with Mid-Nebraska PRIDE?**
Ron Scholey, who was the outgoing leader of Mid-Nebraska PRIDE, came up with the idea to start raising chickens in a different way. He had an organic farm and was operating it like community supported agriculture (**CSA**). Myself and a few of the other farmers got to looking around, saying, "Here we have cattle and hogs. We're more qualified to raise those. Why aren't we selling those, too?" And so we formed North Star Neighbors. Now four or five farms are contributing.

**Was there any agreement or commitment within North Star Neighbors about the quality of the meat or how the animals were going to be raised?**
Yep. We knew that we didn't want to feed the animals antibiotics. We knew we had to be different. Because if we were going to condemn big industry, the big hog guys, then we had to say, "Well, we can't do the same thing." We didn't want to consume [those chemicals], so why would our customers? We started asking a lot of questions about feed ingredients. That kind of set up the standards of what we wanted to be. Our animals aren't fed any **GMOs**.

**Was that a big learning curve?**
From the raising part to the processing part to the marketing part—we learned the whole thing. We developed a delivery system whereby instead of sending four people to a farmers' market in Omaha, three to Lincoln, and one or two to Grand Island, we narrowed that down to one person taking the orders, packaging the orders, and delivering those orders door-to-door. But with the high price of fuel, we came to the point where that wasn't sustainable either. So about three years ago, we formed the Nebraska Food Cooperative.

Pages 18–19:
Knopik's son and partner, Ron, and family move the herd across the road to fresher pasture for the night.

**Tell me about the Nebraska Food Cooperative.**
What this **co-op** does is allow us to work together on developing the distribution system—the system of bringing all of our products together, buying and selling them. The **co-op** does all the invoicing; the folks at the **co-op** buy from the producers, write the checks, and gather the income from the consumers.

**How many producers do you imagine will be tied into the co-op?**
Right now we have sixty, and when this distribution system gets in place, and as people learn about it, that number is going to grow very fast. We have schools, such as the University of Nebraska, that are looking for local food now, plus restaurants and grocery stores. But they don't want to buy from twenty different producers and write twenty different checks. So if they want three hundred pounds of, let's say, potatoes, there are producers out here who can [each] supply fifty pounds, and the **co-op** will put it all together. We're creating opportunity that's going to just keep on growing.

**Have you ever spent much time looking at the Federal Farm Bill?**
Not in detail. I've used the Farm Bill and the farm programs a lot throughout my farming career. The Farm Bill—and I'll put this very bluntly, as clear as I can—is like a bull with a ring in its nose. The Farm Bill leads the farmers in whichever direction big industry wants them to go. If the Farm Bill is set up by big industry, or the big packers, or whoever has the most influence, then that's the direction the farmers will go. And that's the direction the farmers are in now in conventional farming. They are where industry and the big guys want them to be.

**Do you think the Farm Bill could be improved?**
I think it'd be rather easy. See, the Farm Bill now is a top-down policy. The problem with policies is that they only state one rule, and everybody has to abide by the same rule. But it could be done differently.

For example, in Nance County we have sandy soil, prime agricultural black dirt, and hilly land. One policy wouldn't do well here. What it takes is local people deciding what the best policies are for where they live. Local people ought to be making local decisions. You can't have someone in Washington make a farm policy that covers cotton farmers, corn farmers, and potato farmers all in the same stroke of the pen.

But I do think it would be best if the change happened through the Farm Bill— a better farm bill. I think it almost has to, because it's so far out of hand. If it isn't going to happen there, I think it's going to be by a revolution.

**Federal Farm Bill**
The federal government of the United States releases a comprehensive policy proposal to guide the work of the United States Department of Agriculture every few years. This policy can have dramatic implications for issues ranging from international trade and food safety to subsidies for farmers and school lunches to nearly every other policy relating to food and farming.

Opposite, top:
Mid-Nebraska PRIDE is the community coalition that kept the meat monopolies out of Nance County during the "Hog Wars" of the 1990s.

Opposite, bottom:
Jim, an expert in getting animals to easily cooperate, shows his grandsons how to load market-ready hogs into a trailer.

I keep having this vision that there's going to be a turnaround, an exodus or whatever you call it. People are going to have to come out of big cities and go back to farms. The farms are going to have to be divided up, and people are going to have to start farming. We're going to have to start working with more by-hand labor. We better get that in place pretty damn quick, or there's going to be a lot of starving people and a lot of commotion going on.

**Where would you like to see your own farm and your own work in five years?**
Well, before I graduated from high school, I'd see farmers working together. We used to split up hay and we'd thrash, harvest, do so many things together. And the farthest anyone had to drive was a mile to have a group of six or ten farmers working together. By the time I was thirty, me and my kids would have to drive four or five miles to have a group of four farmers working together. Now, it's only our family working, because now you have to drive eight or ten miles to work cooperatively with another farmer. You don't have those close bonds with neighbors anymore: eating together and living together and playing and working and all that. That's pretty much gone.

If I could do it in five years, which might not happen that quickly, I would like to see a farmer on at least every quarter in this area, or maybe every eighty acres. And I think it's real possible, if farmers could generate most of their living off their farm, to meet their needs of eating. We're not going to need as many fossil fuels with communities that are closer together.

And we must change the tax—that's my next deal, really. Because taxation could actually drive the rest of the farmers who are sustainable off their farms if they still can't generate enough money to pay taxes.

**Are you interested in moving in the organics direction?**
At one time I thought this was the way to go, because the organic market is a premium market. The big guys have found a way to tunnel into that market and, by name only, once they [conformed to] the national organic standards, they diluted the organic name—"organic" doesn't mean as much to consumers as it used to. It used to be if something was certified organic, you didn't have to look any further than that, but now [the big companies have] ruined that standard. . . . So nowadays it's more about local foods, and it's not so important to be certified organic.

**Organic food vs. local food**
Ten years ago the idea of organic (produced without nonorganic pesticides, herbicides, and insecticides, or, in the case of animals, raised with restrictions on the administration of antibiotics and hormones) was obscure, but now it's a $20-billion-a-year industry and growing.

As with anything that evolves from a marginal position to a prominent one, debates over definitions of the term and regulations of its use have come from every direction. Many critics claim that the government's certification program favors large corporations and that as more large-scale and international business interests have entered the industry, the word "organic" has lost its meaning.

Alongside the explosion of interest in organic food, the tradition of buying food from local and regional farms, and eating within the season that they are grown, has reemerged in the debates about where our food comes from and who produces it. Organic and local are pitted against one another. Critics argue that while the term "organic" is dubious and communicates little about the social and economic justice aspects of food production (sometimes called fair or direct trade) or the amount of fuel used in transporting food, the term "local" clearly communicates the trend of buying local foods at farmers' markets and through small-scale distributors, giving the eater a more direct connection to the farmer.

Top, left:
Jim and Ron Knopik have two hundred head of grass-fed black angus.

Top, right:
Dean "Whitey" Johnson butchers chickens in the mobile meat-processing facility for North Star Neighbors.

Bottom, left:
Jim's octagenarian mom, Latrice, still helps out in the kitchen of the family's "Loup River Inn."

Bottom, right:
Ron and his wife, Gail, in the side yard with their kids Lane, Jennifer, Ellie, Kyle, and Lexy.

When Whole Foods Market was out in California, the son of their vice president came out and visited with a bunch of our farmers. [The company] wanted to start buying from us. And when they got done interviewing us, and with our meetings, we found out that all they wanted was our story—they didn't care about how the animals were actually raised. They wanted to put the animals out in a big feed lot in western Nebraska where they would all be fed the same rations and bred the same, so that they'd have consistency in the product. That's one thing about local markets or local people selling product: When we raise and produce a finished product, it's not consistent in size or shape or anything like that. But that's what [Whole Foods] was after. They wanted to put our names and our pictures on their package, but they didn't really give a shit about raising them our way. It was all about marketing.

Opposite, top left:
At the corner of Nebraska
Highway 22 and North Star
Road, you'll find the edge of
Jim's property and the North
Star Neighbors sign.

Opposite, top right:
The vast Ogallala aquifer, the
largest underground body of
water in North America, flows
below all of Nebraska. Above
ground, the land is crisscrossed
with creeks and flat rivers.
Here, a lazy finger of the Loup
River flows near Fullerton.

Opposite, bottom:
Jim guides his flock of turkeys
into their home for the night.

Above:
Jim and his dad, Eddie, a
lifelong farmer in Fullerton.

# Greeno Acres

Location:
**Kendall, Wisconsin**

Organizing body:
**1 farmer, with occasional
assistance from friends and family**

Scale:
**160 acres of pasture**

Type:
**For profit**

Currently producing:
**Raw milk**

In operation:
**Since 1993**

Web sites:
**Family Farm Defenders:
familyfarmdefenders.org**

**National Family Farm Coalition:
nffc.net**

**Via Campesina International:
viacampesina.org**

Third-generation Wisconsin dairy farmer Joel Greeno
has been farming for more than fifteen years and
is the current president of the American Raw Milk
Producers Pricing Association (ARMPPA), an organization of dairy farmers dedicated to establishing
a raw-milk price that returns to dairy producers their
cost of production plus a profit.

Greeno is also the vice president of Family Farm
Defenders, the founder of the Scenic Central Milk
Producers Cooperative, and serves on the executive
committee of the **National Family Farm Coalition
(NFFC)** as a representative of ARMPPA. **NFFC** is the
U.S. branch of **La Via Campesina,** the largest farmer
organization in the world. These folks make translocal
connections between their Wisconsin life and peasant
farmers all over the world, often traveling to farmer
summits in Europe and Latin America.

Greeno participates in protests and advocacy for
farmers' rights while maintaining a head of forty dairy
cows. On top of it all, he steals time to participate in
tractor pulls with his friends on the weekends.

Opposite, top:
Between milking, Joel Greeno
spends hours on the phone
networking.

Opposite, bottom:
A three-generation Wisconsin
dairy family: Dad Julian Greeno
at the front; Joel and wife
Laura Greeno, their two-year-
old daughter, Abigail (Abby),
in the middle; and Laura's
brother Tim Ewers on the left.

# Interview with Joel Greeno

**Did you grow up on a dairy farm?**

**Joel Greeno, founder**: Oh, yeah. I've been milking cows since I was ten years old. But ever since I could walk I was in the barn, doing chores of some kind, or feeding cows or calves. During harvest season, I was bailing hay and unloading hay and mowing hay. I spent all summer putting it up and all winter feeding it up. I bought this place in 1990 and then brought cattle here in '93. Been farming here ever since.

**Could you say a little bit about the land and the context here?**

There are a lot of traditional family farms here, and a lot of these farmers pasture one single lot that's used continuously throughout the summer. But I do rotational grazing, whereby you rotate the cow every few days throughout individual managed paddocks. This way, there isn't as much fuel going through tractors and equipment, and I cut down on fossil fuel too by not using commercial fertilizers. I'm probably looked at as the oddball because of that.

**What motivated you to attend your first meeting around farmer activist work?**

In October 1996, "Black Friday" happened: Farmers' milk prices dropped six dollars a hundredweight over a two-month period—almost a 30 percent drop at the time. It left all farmers in an income crunch, struggling to pay bills. People's parents were getting put out of business. I began to wonder, "Why?"

In February '97, I was invited to a meeting of the American Raw Milk Producers Pricing Association. I met John Kinsman, Francis Goodman, and other longtime farmer-activists with the Family Farm Defenders; joined the organization; and eighteen months later I became president.

Initially, I set up small local meetings but never really spoke to a crowd—just arranged things, introduced people, let them handle it. But in September of that same year, my grandfather passed away at eighty-eight years old. From his funeral, I got in a van and drove all the way to upstate New York, where I was told I would be the opening speaker in front of four hundred farmers. I had some major butterflies, but I told my family's story, talked about my grandfather's passing, how we were all in this together, that milk prices weren't fair, and that we could work together to fix it. A lot of people got choked up. But people came together. We created a good, solid organization.

**Black Friday**

For nearly eighty years, every Friday at 10 A.M. traders representing the dairy industry would meet for one half hour on the floor of the National Cheese Exchange (NCE) in Green Bay, Wisconsin. In 1996, between October and December, cheese prices fell dramatically, leaving dairy farmers with huge cuts in their monthly incomes. The start of this decline on November 1 was known to dairy farmers as "Black Friday," resulting in a loss of three dollars for every hundred pounds ("hundredweight") of milk sold that month.

Historically the NCE had a huge impact on the cheese industry, with the vast majority of wholesale cheese being sold through its infrastructure. Even as its role in selling cheese declined, its role shifted toward influencing milk prices by swaying the Basic Formula Price used by the United States Department of Agriculture as the foundation for all milk prices. In 1997 the NCE closed its doors, and the commodity trading associated with the dairy industry moved to the Chicago Mercantile Exchange.

Opposite, top:
A Wisconsin sunset.

Opposite, bottom:
Joel Greeno and John Peck (in cow suit), president of Family Farm Defenders, share a light moment after a protest at the county fair in La Crosse, Wisconsin.

**What led you to establish the Scenic Central Milk Producers Cooperative?**
I recruited a group of farmers who'd agreed to be the interim directors of the **co-op**, and they filed the articles of incorporation. We were naive to think we could have a **co-op** up and running in a month or two—we ended up fighting state of Wisconsin red tape for ten months to obtain all of our permits and inspections.

In ten years' time, we were able to grow from the smallest **co-op** in the United States to the fortieth largest in the country. We're very successful in what we do: marketing farmers' milk, paying top prices, providing excellent services, providing retirement plans in the form of Roth IRAs, Christmas bonuses . . . things to benefit farmers.

**What inspired you to join so many organizations and coalitions?**
Meeting John Kinsman and also becoming a member of the American Raw Milk Producers (ARMPPA)—and eventually becoming the vice president. Through that organization and Family Farm Defenders, we look at the whole picture; we know we're not going to fix the milk situation by just dealing with milk. Everything is interwoven, and in order to save dairy farmers, we have to look at all farmers and take on the actions to protect all farmers, whether they are milking cows, organic or conventional, or raising corn and beans.

That's the nice part of the **National Family Farm Coalition**: You have a wide range of almost forty farm organizations coming together under a common banner, sharing their problems, and supporting each other. Through the **NFFC**, we found that contract poultry growers were some of the earliest hit by corporate agriculture, in that you owned a farm but basically owned nothing else. The big corporations would come and say, "We'll build you facilities, we'll provide you with feed, we'll provide you with chickens, you raise those chickens, and then you sell those chickens to us, and this is how much you will make." But they don't tell you that if one bird dies, you have to pay for it. Then it went to hogs, then cattle, and dairy was last.

**How do commodity brokers and financial spectators affect the price that you get for milk?**
There is near direct correlation between what farmers get paid for raw milk and the forty-pound cheddar price on the Chicago Mercantile Exchange, where agricultural commodities are bought, traded, and sold. That cheese market is not supposed to have any impact on my milk market. There is lots of talk that "it's

**Chicago Mercantile Exchange (CME)**
Often called "The Merc," this institution was founded in 1898 as the Chicago Butter and Egg Board, solidifying its deep connections to the food industry's evolution. Here the financial representation of raw materials such as metals and agricultural commodities (not the plants and animals themselves!) are bought and sold, in addition to trading in "futures and options on futures" based on interest rates, equity indexes, foreign exchange, energy, and alternative investment products, such as weather and real estate. In recent years the Merc has merged with the Chicago Board of Trade and the New York Mercantile Exchange, making it the largest options and futures market in the world. The financialization of agricultural (and industrial) economies like that of the United States has contributed to the growing disconnect between consumers and the production process—most people care more about food prices than they do about food production simply because the production has been able to literally happen further and further away from the point of trade, pricing, and selling.

supply and demand," but if you take a milk supply line and put it on a graph, and put the dairy farmers' pay price on that same graph, you have a slow, steady, 1.4 average increase per year in milk production, and farmers' pay price looks like a heart monitor. There is no correlation.

You basically have a triangle of three that control every aspect of the dairy industry: Kraft Foods, which controls 40 percent of the cheese market; Dean Foods, which controls 40 percent of the fluid market; and Grassland [Dairy Products] in butter. Each has their turf, and nobody interferes on their turf.

**What impact has international networking had on you?**
**National Family Farm Coalition** is affiliated with the international network of **La Via Campesina**. It makes me feel a little stronger knowing that I have people in other countries who support me, who are fighting the same fight, and, in a lot of cases, we are fighting a common enemy: multinational, transnational companies that are using each country's unique situation to basically control markets worldwide. We are exposing that by all working altogether.

Those of us who organize here have been extremely impressed with the Movimento dos Trabalhadores Rurais Sem Terra (MST), the landless peasant workers movement in Brazil, and with just how committed they are to the movement. They face being killed, at gunpoint, and still continue the movement even under the worst odds, the worst conditions. They make you hope to someday have that level of commitment. MST has done so much more with less. We need to step it up here. There's some of us who joke that organizing farmers is kind of like herding cats or trying to keep frogs in a wheelbarrow: You put three in and two escape.

**In what ways would you like to see progressive land reform happen in the United States?**
Well, it's always been a good thing that farmers have owned land, but today, most of the land isn't owned by the people farming it. It's rented land bought out by companies and real estate brokers and developers. That kind of removes the personal touch, meaning you don't have the respect for that land as if it were your own. And it tends to lead to management decisions that aren't in the best interest of food concerns or quality of food—you get into the issues of genetically modified crops, soybeans, and even into the issue of patenting life. Does **Monsanto** have the right to say, "We now own corn"? Is that right?

Top, left:
Joel Greeno speaks to the
media after a big rally in West
La Crosse, Wisconsin. The rally
was for fair organic pricing to
meet the cost of production,
and to protest the consolidation of organic dairies that
bypasses organic standards.

Top, right:
Greeno approaches Tom
Vilsack, U.S. Secretary of
Agriculture for the Obama
administration, after the rally.

Bottom:
Greeno uses his four-wheeler
to move cows to a new grazing
location.

Right:
Any seat will do.

**Dairy Farmers of America**
Formed in 1998 through the
merger of four large regional
cooperatives, the DFA is the
largest milk marketing cooperative in the country. This
cooperative of more than ten
thousand farms has been sued
by farmers several times for
monopolistic behavior in col-
lusion with other giants in the
dairy industry, such as Dean
Foods and Dairy Marketing
Services. In 2008, DFA was
fined by the Commodity
Futures Trading Commission
for attempting to manipulate
cheddar cheese prices at the
Chicago Mercantile Exchange
in 2004 in order to affect
the price of milk futures prices.
The link between cheese
futures at the CME and milk
prices is known in the industry
and ripe to be exploited by
those with significant buying
power.

**How can different sectors of agriculture, and specifically dairy, strike a balance between large- and small-scale operations that work?**

Dairy Farmers of America is so big and powerful that it's able to control markets, cheat markets, and even break the law. You get to be so big that you're not really held accountable. Our plan with ARMPPA is to have a series of small-run **co-ops** that work for a select group of farmers and work together through **marketing agencies in common**. We try to complement and protect one another, not be the big bully on the block. We do everything by cooperation and in the best interest of the farmer and the consumer. We keep things balanced to avoid creating an environment where you benefit by an upswing or a downswing.

**Where would you like to see farmers in five years?**

I'd like to see more family farms on the land. I'd like to see farmers working together better. Wisconsin used to be covered with successful, small, family cheese operations. We don't need extreme consolidation in the marketplace; we don't need plant closures; we don't need central, larger facilities, because more, smaller facilities will employ more people over a greater area.

Corporate agriculture is not in it for quality. They're not looking out for the consumer or the farmer; they're just in it to make money, pure and simple.

People need to recognize the fact that there are only four sources of the world's raw material: agriculture, forestry, aquaculture, and mining. Agriculture is 70 percent of all raw material. Farmers are absolutely vital, because it's kind of hard to eat oil or trees; fish is okay, but there is only so much. No matter what, everybody's got to eat every day or our days are numbered. That's it in a nutshell.

Opposite, top:
High school student and
neighbor Brandon Scott (front)
is Joel and Julian's much-
appreciated hired hand.

Opposite, bottom left:
Fresh, raw, organic milk as it
comes from the barn to the
collection room.

Opposite, bottom right:
Greeno leaves the house and
heads for work with Missy
the dog.

Above:
Greeno is "mowing" (stacking)
the hay in the hay mow. It's
hard work but one of his
favorite jobs on the farm.

# IN INTENTIONAL COMMUNITY

# Sandhill Community Farm

Location:
**Rutledge, Missouri**

Organizing body:
**6 adults and 1 thirteen-year-old child, plus rotating interns**

Scale:
**135 acres (15 acres of farmland, 60 acres of grassland, and 60 acres of woodland)**

Type:
**For profit, certified organic**

Currently producing:
**Sorghum, wheat, honey, garlic, mustard, and horseradish**

In operation:
**Since 1974**

Web site:
**sandhillfarm.org**

For more than thirty years, Sandhill Community Farm has been an intentional community farm built around **biodynamic**, cooperative, and egalitarian principals. The folks at Sandhill grow food for their own consumption, as well as for sale in markets and as processed "**value added**" products such as jams, salsas, and their own line of sorghum goods (which they celebrate each fall with a harvest festival). They have prioritized self-sufficiency, raising more than 80 percent of their own food, including the difficult task of harvesting and processing their own grains. The group grapples with an approach to appropriate technologies for their time and context—opting, for example, to use a fuel-based tractor but to do most of the farming by hand. Recently they completed their own eco-audit to more precisely evaluate the strengths and weaknesses of their consumption and production practices.

The group has changed and evolved since its inception in 1974. In 1979, they were looking to become connected to other groups across the country who pooled their incomes and thereby joined the Federation of Egalitarian Communities. Around 1989 the group decided to become the headquarters for the world-renowned Fellowship of Intentional Communities, which publishes a magazine and directory about communal living. Many of the aging members have taken jobs off the farm and become involved in the broader community. Others have gotten heavily involved in activism trying to keep **CAFOs** (Concentrated Animal Feeding Operations) from entering their county.

# Interview with Stan Hildebrand, Gigi Wahba, and Käthe Nicosia

**How would you describe this region?**

**Stan Hildebrand, community member**: It's a hilly region with deciduous forests. Farms are smaller compared to others in the United States, anywhere from two hundred to one thousand acres. People grow corn, soybeans, and beef cattle since the land is hilly and more suitable to pasture. It's very, very rural. Very few people live here. A lot of Mennonites have moved into the area in the last twenty years. They compose roughly a third of the population and more than half of the farmers in the county.

**Gigi Wahba, community member**: Few people grow their own food anymore, even though they are farmers and they grew up eating food from gardens. There aren't many organic farmers. We are definitely the minority. But there is a strong sense of community—quality of life and pride. There are multigenerations of the same family living within a hundred miles of each other. We don't have a Walmart. And there aren't any stoplights in the whole county.

**Talk about your internal economy, sharing resources between yourselves, and also the external economy of having a business.**

**SH**: Sandhill Farm started in 1974. When I came in '79, we were trying to earn all of our income from agricultural sources—we did the sorghum business, started honey, and managed various other businesses. Year after year we had a shortfall. The only way we stayed afloat was because several people gave or loaned money to the community, money that they had inherited or come by. Fifteen years after I joined, we finally balanced our budget and realized [that another reason we survived] was because two people in the community did outside work. One was a massage therapist and the other was a piano teacher. It just kind of brought it home, at least to me, that our model wasn't working. We had to let go of that model of making it agriculturally.

Ever since then, more and more of our income has come from off-farm money than on-farm products. Costs keep going up, yet we're not able to increase prices [at the same rate], and so, luckily, we have these outside streams of income from jobs that people enjoy doing.

**Intentional community**
A group of people typically living (sometimes just working) together with a unifying, shared vision. This catchall term applies to some religious and spiritual communities, eco-villages, and groups of people banned together because of a political belief. The practice is frequently adopted by people who want to live differently from the dominant currents of society. Joining a community can involve varying paths, yet since most of them require significant reliance on the other people, it is important that trust and transparency be achieved between newcomers and those already "in community." The Fellowship of Intentional Communities publishes a community magazine and directory, which is an excellent source for finding out more about the world of intentional communities.

Above:
The group prepares for dinner with a song.

**GW**: Internally, we're kind of Marxist. To each according to their need, and from each according to their ability. We operate with a high level of trust between us. Our lives intersect a lot here. Basically, when you become a member, you get the privilege of writing checks. When people have expenses, they generally feel free to pay for them. We keep track of where everything goes, and we can count every dollar spent, every income that's come in. There's no joining fee, and generally, when you are here, whatever work you do goes toward the common pool. When you leave, often the community will give you a leaving fund.

**What bodies of ecology and food production thought do you subscribe to?**
**GW**: Because there's so many people involved here, we're not real rigid about one particular methodology. Mostly we're growing soil. We are trying to increase fertility and productivity in all our soils, in the gardens, in the fields. We bring in insects, create microclimates that are favorable, maintain the natural habitats. Organic, **biodynamic**, **permaculture**, holistic field-management practices—all of that fits in.

**SH**: We try to make use of what we have here and circulate those resources rather than be dependent on outside resources. That can be Native American, it can be **biodynamic**, or it can be **fukuoka**. It is very eclectic.

**How do you deal with waste here?**

**Käthe Nicosia, community member**: We recycle everything we possibly can, use up everything we can. For the stuff that isn't recyclable, we have a small landfill, and we try to manage it intelligently.

**Is there a story to how the Sandhill family of products came about?**

**SH**: We started with one product, which was sorghum, a long time ago. We started going to fairs, and then we added honey. After a while we realized that if we're going to be sitting there at the table all day long, we could be selling ten products. So we started adding more and more things: mustard, horseradish, one after another. It was trial and error.

**GW**: Growing these gardens all these years, there's always something that does phenomenal. Oftentimes, it's tomatoes and peppers. We've taken the attitude that we'll work with whatever we've got.

**KN**: The products are also driven by people's interests, what we want to put energy into. There's a lot in the condiment line now: sauces, relishes, chutneys.

**How does the division of labor work?**

**KN**: We stay focused on what needs to be done. Some of our work is definitely very seasonal. Every member has a different mix of things they do—we don't all do exactly the same thing. But all of us are expected to harvest sorghum. Those doing garden work must also routinely walk around the garden so that everyone is informed about what is going on with each crop and what harvests are coming up.

**SH**: We all take turns cooking and cleaning the house—we divide up chores, whether it's washing windows or washing floors. You get one area that you may do for a whole year, or you might do it for a few months and switch with someone. All of us like a lot of variation in our daily routine—a lot of times you don't know what you are going to be doing that day when you get up, but you get to decide. People who want a more regular routine and know what their entire week looks like probably wouldn't fit here.

**KN**: We tend to self-select for self-starters. You've got to be motivated to get yourself going. Nobody's going to push you out the door.

**GW**: Another dynamic here is that the oldest members have taken a greater interest in things outside of Sandhill Farm. We all have outside jobs in addition to the daily chores. The community has had to evolve with that. For instance, you join a

Top, left:
The entranceway to the farm.

Top, right:
Storage tanks and bottles for
Sandhill products.

Bottom, left:
The sorghum mill.

Bottom, right:
Sandhill Farm maintains
gardens for daily use as well
as fields for larger crops.

community at a certain phase of your life, then your interests change, and then you change. Can the community continue to support that? Sandhill's been around for thirty years, and if the community's going to go forward, we need young people who are going to do the day-to-day work and take on the management and that kind of thing. As always, we're in transition.

**Where would you all like to see Sandhill in five years?**
**GW**: I like what we're doing now! I'd hope we'd get people who'd like to continue what we're doing now. I hope we keep growing our food.

**SH**: I'd love to be part of the local-foods movement. If it means doing stuff with neighboring intentional communities or starting a local farmers' market in Memphis, that'd be awesome.

**KN**: I think our initiative to start our own farmers' market in the nearby town has some possibilities of turning into something pretty good, for both the local area and the local communities. That's been pretty exciting to me—it's been a high point of my year.

# Tryon Life Community Farm

Location:
**Portland, Oregon**

Organizing body:
**15 adults and 3 children**

Scale:
**7 acres**

Type:
**Nonprofit, intentional community**

Currently producing:
**Echinacea, red chili peppers**

In operation:
**Since 2004**

Web site:
**tryonfarm.org**

Opposite, top:
An overview of the land and
surrounding Tryon Creek
State Park.

Opposite, bottom:
(From left) Chelle Webster
(John's visiting sister); Ember
Summer; Chad Dermann;
Laura Dvorak; Brenna Bell
with baby Raven Summer, two
weeks old; Maggie Simon;
and John Brush (Brenna's
partner).

Situated within a 650-acre ecosystem of towering firs, cedars, and diverse Northwest forest known as Tryon Creek State Park is a clearing dotted with small rustic dwellings, outdoor kitchenettes, and a sweat lodge. Although the setting suggests a fairy tale, the members of Tryon Life Community (TLC) Farm are not after an escape. Instead, they offer a potent demonstration of functional alternatives.

In 2004, the plot was rescued from being developed into twenty-three minimansions. TLC raised $1.6 million through a grassroots campaign to buy the land from the developer. The proposed transition of the land from private to public was carried by the local press and strongly supported by the larger community, because the campaign embodied issues of land use and zoning that affect the daily lives of Portlanders. The land they bought as a joint effort with the Oregon Sustainable Agricultural Land Trust (OSALT) keeps them connected to land-use policy and stands as a model for a less speculative approach to real estate.

Eighteen people live on the nonprofit farm in an intentional community called Cedar Moon, which is a counterpart to TLC Farm. Residents volunteer ten hours per week to maintain the land, work on building projects, and conduct educational workshops, events, outreach, and spiritual ecology. Another six hours per week are contributed to the communal household through cooking, cleaning, other chores, and gardening. Their outreach and activism ranges from distributing Tryon Hot Cock Sauce, their own brand of locally popular hot sauce, to working with Oregon Recode, an initiative to reform various zoning laws to be more socially and ecologically progressive.

# Interview with Brenna Bell and Bonsai Matt James

**LEED certification**
Leadership in Energy and Environmental Design is an internationally recognized green building certification system, providing third-party verification that a building or community was designed and built using strategies aimed at improving performance in energy savings, water efficiency, $CO_2$ emissions reduction, improved indoor environmental quality, and stewardship of resources and sensitivity to their impacts.

**Tell us about this site and its relation to the surrounding Portland area.**
**Brenna Bell, member, environmental lawyer, and activist**: TLC Farm is located in the Tryon Creek watershed, which is a direct tributary to the Willamette River. Midway between the Cascade Mountains and the Pacific Ocean, the native habitat is temperate evergreen forest dominated by Western red cedar, Douglas fir, and Western hemlock, with deciduous big-leaf maple and red alder. The native people of this land were the Kalapuya and the Tualitin tribes, who were people of the salmon.

Portland is now known for its progressive approach to city planning and sustainability. It has a mostly liberal, white population that prides itself on doing things more environmentally sensitive than in other cities—even though we are still overly dependent on fossil fuels, imported foods, et cetera. The city helps rather than hinders creative approaches to sustainability. However, the dominant trend is toward sustainable solutions that are part of the "green economy" for example, LEED-certified houses and other high-tech green solutions. TLC Farm is pushing the city's boundaries with our DIY approach.

**Bonsai Matt James, member and Bonsai Nursery owner**: We're in southwest Portland. This land was named for Thaddeus Tryon, who was responsible for protecting this piece of forest homestead about seventy years ago. The land has changed so many times in the last forty years or so that this field has seen various states of intense cultivation and disrepair. It still needs a lot in terms of drainage and organic matter.

**What was the campaign to save this land like?**
**BB**: We called it "creating a buzz." At the time, it was a very private place—a hippie-party-artist-farmer–law student rental place. I moved here in 2000 as a law student. When we got the eviction notice, we made a big deal about how we weren't going to leave, which got a great article in the *Oregonian*. We had to come up with a million and a half dollars in ten months, so we created a big buzz. We did a tremendous amount of outreach and started doing a lot of programming—children's programs, tours—making it a public space so that we would have something to point the public to. We canvassed everywhere around the neighborhood, had picnics, kept doing media, trying to get the story out there. In the end we needed to raise $200,000 in ten days. It was a total media blitz.

Opposite, top:
Mothers drop off their children for a day at the rural oasis in the middle of urban Portland.

Opposite, bottom:
The community's beloved sweat lodge and barn.

**Can you tell us a bit about your relationship to the surrounding 650-acre Tryon Creek State Park?**

**BB**: There is a buffer zone. When we purchased the land we put it into a land trust. We were able to help secure it with money from the government that went toward buying a conservation easement on the buffer between the farm and the park. By the terms of the easement, we can't have conventional gardens in the buffer, but we are not super-keen on conventional farming anyway, so we are looking at how to build food forests—food-producing plants—in the buffer zone. In the buffer, all plants have to be native; as we move away from the buffer we can have more nonnative forests. That is our way of stacking functions, so we are simultaneously preserving the wildlife habitat and creating food-producing ecosystems.

**What got you inspired? What got you into growing food?**

**BM**: Ever since I was a kid I realized that things were going wrong with the world and that food shortage and food production were big issues. It used to be that one in ten people were growing food for their surrounding community. Now it is more like one in a hundred or two hundred. It won't be possible to transport food the way we've been. It's a total luxury that we have. During the last ten years I was thinking about how and where to start an urban **demonstration project**, and . . . now we've got real food production happening and a **CSA** (Community Supported Agriculture) operation going along with our educational aspect.

**Do you connect yourself to other initiatives?**

**BM**: We work with Pacific Crest Community High School, an alternative school that holds class here once a week. The students learn how to farm and garden, how to cook and tend animals, and how to communicate and be with one another. We also work with the People's Co-op in town to get our food sold there.

**Can you talk about Recode Oregon?**

**BB**: My pet project has been taking on regulatory barriers to sustainable practices. This year we organized a statewide campaign to legalize the use of gray water, which is not legal in Oregon. We just got legislation signed and passed by the governor. Now we are talking to the city of Portland about changing its zoning laws that prohibit small-scale commercial gardening on residential lots.

We are also trying to redefine the definition of a "household." The current definition limits it to a lot with five unrelated adults. We are trying to redefine that to allow for more shared housing with different land-use and building codes. For instance, encouraging the use of local, minimally processed materials and having multiple small structures on a piece of land rather than one large dwelling. People are doing this anyway, but we can't promote it as widely if it's illegal. TLC Farm started Recode Oregon, which has taken off as the driving force behind a lot of this, together with many community members, including the Northwest EcoBuilding Guild.

**What aspect of TLC are you most excited about?**
**BM**: I am focusing on a few important medicines. I think it's important to grow medicines locally so that they process the same pollutants in the air, have the same things in the ground, and basically share the same environment with the people whom they will be helping. We have a few patches of really potent medicinal plants that we feed our own pee and spit, wash our feet near, to give it the DNA downloads of ourselves so that the medicines will be customized for exactly what we need. Some of those are echinacea, valerian, thyme, and oregano, which are overlooked medicinal plants in this day and age.

**What unique methods do you employ to help you here?**
**BM**: We like collecting cardboard. We get them out of the Dumpsters every few weeks. We cut our grass and lay cardboard over it to kill the grass; later it decomposes to create soil. It's a great option rather than tilling. We also use old carpets to cover the ground—it's so much easier to get in and dig in the ground. If [we suspect that] the carpets or cardboard are leaching toxins into the ground, we inoculate our whole garden with mushrooms. Mushrooms act as a biofilter, processing any toxins or poisonous residues from the glues used to make cardboard and from fire retardants in carpet. Mushrooms can process many types of poisonous toxins. We use oyster, shiitake, *Stropharia rugosoa annulata* or white cap mushrooms, and a few others.

**What do you grow or raise?**
**BM**: We have two hives of bees. I stack straw bales around them for shelter in the winter to keep them alive. We have goats for milk and cheese that we make here, sheep for wool and as lawn mowers, and chickens for eggs. The bees are pollinators.

We grow all the common veggies. We try not to grow the staples of grain and potatoes because they take up too much space. So we grow mostly veggies and medicinal plants. Our small nursery brings in money, too.

**Do members have other jobs or does the farm sustain everyone?**
**BM**: Everyone here has [an outside] job and earns whatever they can. We all pay the mortgage, which we split. Workshops bring in a good amount of money, but we're always trying to get donations to pay off the land.

**Where do you see TLC Farm in five years?**

**BB**: As a place for people to learn the skills necessary to create a new, truly sustainable world. The whole array of skills: from **permaculture** and natural building to leading Earth ceremonies and consensus meetings.

I'd also like to see it as a place where people can immerse in the natural world without retreating from the city, and to re-create what a city can look like—integrating human habitat, wild habitat, and food production. A place where people can remember that all our ancestors, once, were indigenous and take steps to reawaken that indigeneity in ourselves. Small change is no longer enough, and we want to help radically shift the nature of the city and its inhabitants. We're using all the different tools of education, demonstration, policy change, et cetera, toward these goals.

Above, left:
Young students enjoy a salad they picked minutes ago.

Above, right:
Tryon resident Matt Bibeau leads a "Right of Passage" summer class for boys, under the eaves of an outdoor kitchen constructed of whole trees.

Opposite, top:
The communal kitchen.

Opposite, bottom:
Summer-camp kids play together.

# City Slicker Farms

Location:
**Oakland, California**

Organizing body:
**4 staff, 3 paid apprentices, and 8 interns, plus multiple volunteers**

Scale:
**3 urban farms, 100+ backyard gardens, and farm stands**

Type:
**Nonprofit**

Currently producing:
**Winter greens and root vegetables**

In operation:
**Since 2000**

Web site:
**cityslickerfarms.org**

"Free Spirit," "Penny Pincher," and "Sugar Mama and Daddy" are price categories at City Slicker Farms' Saturday farm stand that sells produce, eggs, and honey on a sliding scale. The organization uses humor as a way to soften the stigma so many times associated with being broke.

Located in the heart of Oakland, California's, West Oakland neighborhood, City Slicker Farms is a nonprofit that is creating healthful resources for its community. West Oakland is an urban district of hardworking residents who are challenged by high crime, low income, and few jobs or other opportunities. The residents have suffered effects of environmental racism; they live with industrial pollutants from the nearby port and manufacturers, and lack easily accessible grocery stores that sell fresh foods.

City Slicker Farms runs farms in six locations in the municipality with four staff, three paid farm apprentices, eight interns, and many volunteers. Emphasis is placed on high-nutrient, high-yield crops such as winter greens and root vegetables. Chickens are raised for eggs, and honey is produced as well. The Backyard Garden Program donates materials and know-how to individual families; it offers those who have a little extra land and the desire to grow food a "sustainable, complementary alternative to food banks and other charity-based emergency food programs." Each year around seventy-five families build a backyard garden through the program.

# Interview with Willow Rosenthal and Barbara Finnin

**How did you get involved in this project?**

**Willow Rosenthal, founder**: I grew up in Sonoma County, California, which is an agricultural area, especially then. My dad was really into gardening. I worked on farms in high school. In college I was looking to do social-justice work, but not looking into agriculture at all. I moved to the San Francisco Bay Area in 1997 and did an internship with **Food First**. I started volunteering with the Organic Consumer Association, an organization working against the **GMO** issue. They were doing a lot of direct-action stuff. One of our favorite actions was dumping a whole dump-truck load of Starlink corn on the **Environmental Protection Agency's** steps in San Francisco.

When I moved to West Oakland, I was taken by all the vacant land. I also noticed that there weren't many grocery stores. My neighbors were buying food at the corner liquor stores and taking the bus [several miles away] to Pak 'n Save in Emeryville. For all the conversations I had about food justice in my previous work, I found myself looking around saying, "This is it."

I decided to get a lot to farm and have it be a community thing. I started asking around and met a Realtor who told me about an auction in Alameda County for tax-defaulted properties. A friend of mine had just inherited some money and agreed to loan me some. Long story short, we went to the auction and got a lot for $11,000.

My intention was to start a community farm, not a community garden, because a community farm has one plan for growing crops and everyone can participate. People can do work-trade. I am all about yields. Little plots with herbs and flowers and a couple vegetables isn't efficient, and people aren't working together.

In this community, people are scrambling to put food on the table, and, let's face it, they probably don't have time to volunteer. I never felt that they should volunteer, I felt that they should participate however they felt they needed to. Some could garden or just come by to get food.

Opposite, top:
Jamori Kelly (left) and Ja'mar Brown (right) pose with the delivery trike.

Opposite, bottom:
Volunteer Don Donahue at West Oakland Woods (WOW) Farm turns compost while a BART train passes in the background.

**At that time was the farm mostly targeted toward growing food for the neighborhood?**

WR: Yes, but there was always an issue about how to work in a community like this one. There is a dilemma about how to make it work without patronizing people. Empowerment comes with the residents gaining control over their food system.

I felt that farming here was a solidarity option. I have a skill and I was willing to bring it to the community and to revalue farming, which, in an African American community, is a big issue given slavery and our history. I tried to convey that what solidarity means is that you are risking something yourself. And the hands-on response from both children and adults has been positive. I always say that gardening is uncontroversial. It's universally uncontroversial.

**How has the local economy impacted your project?**

WR: The local economy was the impetus for the project. While people may own their homes, they might not be able to maintain them. There are no jobs, the school system is horrible, and people live on really low, often fixed incomes. We know from our questionnaires that they live on $10,000 a year.

**Can you tell us about the Backyard Garden Program?**

WR: We ask recipients of the Backyard Garden Program to donate five hours of time to the organization every year, but we don't check up on it. We want them to come to the farms to see how different things are done. It's free for low-income residents of West Oakland. The income requirements are based on HUD [U.S. Department of Housing and Urban Development]. People with middle or high incomes pay a graduated amount. We have one staff member who runs the Back-yard Garden Program. We have two core groups of volunteers: builders and mentors.

In order for something to change in your habit life, you need a lot of support, and if we don't provide the support, we're going to have a lot of lean planter boxes a year from now. We require the family to be there. We bring materials. We install it all together, and then the mentor comes to connect. We recruit mentors from the participants. That's how the knowledge passes on.

**Can you tell us a bit about the nuts and bolts of the project: fertilizing, waste, distribution?**

WR: We use compost to fertilize. Since we use the **biointensive method**, compost is a huge deal in terms of replenishing the soil to keep it nutrient rich. We use on-site waste, and we have a bicycle route that picks up our neighbors' compost.

**Oakland Food Policy Council**

The OFPC is a coalition of organizations that was approved by the city of Oakland in 2006 to advocate policies and programs that eliminate the root causes of hunger, increase the number of food-sector living-wage jobs in Oakland, and help create a sustainable and localized food system whereby up to 30 percent of Oakland's food is grown locally and food businesses drastically curb their waste.

We would like to do this on a larger scale, but city permitting is an issue. We use fish emulsion when necessary. In terms of waste, we try to close the loop whenever possible. For example, we take our rotting garden beds to the dump to be made into wood chips. As for distribution, every Saturday if there is any extra food, we bike around the neighborhood and give it away. This is a really positive marketing tool that helps with the organization's goal of meeting people where they live.

**Do you receive funds or loans?**
**Barbara Finnin, director**: As with all nonprofits, diversity of funds is essential. We receive money from foundations, individuals, corporations, and the sale of produce. In-kind donations are huge and enable us to use the resources that already exist in our community.

**Food touches on so many aspects of political life. Has your project affected any local policies or changed city policy?**
**BF**: We work with many groups. We advocate for policies that make urban agriculture easier, for instance, zoning for farming and water access. There are already policies in place for community gardening and parks but not necessarily about intensely growing food as a priority for the city.

**WR**: It's really difficult, because you can feel stretched too thin to focus on policy. Eventually you find out that [the government] doesn't allow something, and then you have to go talk to the law makers. [After some battle,] we were able to get the city council to approve an Oakland Food Policy Council. As a result of this, we received $100,000 from the city of Oakland to create a model project using underutilized parks to grow food.

**City Slicker Farms' Web site states that environmental racism is a daily reality in West Oakland. Can you explain that?**
**WR**: In terms of environmental racism, there are many examples you can look at that are true in all major cities throughout the country. Many neighborhoods were [designated as] mixed-use for industry and residences because they were near railroads or a port. In those situations, you have a lot of contamination from the past that was never cleaned up, or you have current industry pollution. The reason I consider it to be environmental racism is because communities that are more black and brown also make up a larger percentage of the lower-income people. The neighborhood here is more than 60 percent African American and about 15 percent Hispanic. There is a very low Asian population, and the remaining population is white or multiracial.

Lower-income people do not have the time to approach, let alone easy access to, the avenues of power and the decision makers. The polluters get away with [their actions] simply because the people, for those reasons, are not able to make a fuss.

**What is the most difficult decision you have had to make?**
**WR**: Honestly, it has been to continue City Slicker Farms. So much of our work has been unbelievably easy. We have hardly ever had to reach out for volunteers or to make sure that the participants we wanted to reach were being reached. It wasn't hard, it was just making an effort. The good will of the community has been so large. [But the problem is that] there's just no money to do this work, and, in a community that needs jobs, the way that you can get work done is to pay people. People have this idea that you can do everything through volunteerism, but there's a certain accountability that comes with being paid, and to run an organization you need that accountability among your staff.

Above:
Vertical demonstration gardens
at Center Street Farm.

Opposite:
Adelle Martin readies the
lettuce for the sliding scale
market table where customers
decide if they are a "Free
Spirit," "Just Getting By," or a
"Sugar Mama/Daddy" and pay
accordingly.

# Angelic Organics Learning Center

Location:
**Caledonia, Chicago,
and Rockford, Illinois**

Organizing body:
**12 staff**

Scale:
**220 acres of farmland, forest,
oak savannah, prairie strips,
orchards, and flowing creeks
in Caledonia, plus additional,
rotating acreage in urban areas
of Chicago and Rockford**

Type:
**Nonprofit wing of
a for-profit farm**

Currently producing:
**New farmers and
gardeners**

In operation:
**Since 1998**

Web site:
**learngrowconnect.org**

The Angelic Organics Learning Center (AOLC) is the nonprofit education and outreach partner of Angelic Organics Farm, one of the largest community supported agriculture (**CSA**) farms in the country. Mostly city folk from Chicago buy "shares" in the farm and get a box of farm-fresh food once a week. So the fruits of the farm itself can be seen on dinner tables and in lunch pails throughout the far-reaching sprawl that is Chicago and its suburbs.

The Learning Center itself, an outgrowth of the **biodynamic** farm and **CSA**, has three main locations and thematic focus areas: the Urban Initiative, which offers support and leadership development to residents of Chicago and Rockford who are trying to create and improve their local food systems; the Farmer Training Initiative, which offers training to new farmers from Angelic Organics Farm in Caledonia, Illinois (roughly two hours from Chicago); and the On-Farm Initiative, which offers education programs ranging from school visits on the farm to food production (organic gardening, wine, cheese, etc.) workshops.

Opposite:
Martha Boyd plants future
deliciousness.

# Interview with Tom Spaulding, Thea Maria Carlson, Martha Boyd, and Sheri Doyel

**The Angelic Organics Learning Center covers a large territory—urban, suburban, and rural. How did that happen?**
**Tom Spaulding, executive director**: When the rural northern Illinois farm we are on went under as a conventional farm in the 1980s, it was reborn as Angelic Organics Farm [for more history, see the independent film *The Real Dirt on Farmer John*], an organic, **biodynamic**, **CSA** farm in Caledonia. We had a strong connection to the urban people who supported this, so when the Learning Center was born in 1999, just six years after the **CSA** started, our natural region enlarged to include Chicago, the rural ring around it, and up into southern Wisconsin. This is because the food system that serves Chicago does not respect county or state lines.

Thus the farm and the Learning Center have relationships with people through our economic, social, and cultural involvements, and these entail linking up with people of all economic levels and cultural backgrounds. We've taken on the shapes, colors, and ideas of people from very diverse backgrounds. There is a diversity of classes, genders, and age, and we are better off for it.

**Thea Maria Carlson, Urban Initiative program coordinator**: In almost every neighborhood in Chicago, there is a pretty big mix of different kinds of people. It's challenging and fun to figure out how to get everyone on the same page about food. But what I love about food is that everyone has to eat!

**What are some of the advantages of working through legislature and government?**
**TS**: Farms at this moment—if they are **biodynamic** or have other natural approaches— are part of the cultural, social, and economic renewal that we need. The advocacy and policy work we do emerges organically from the people we're working with, from what they're involved in and are facing in their lives. For instance, we started working with people who want to raise chickens in the city, when all of a sudden the city said that chickens should be banned because they're a health hazard. It was almost imperative that we got involved. We are not a big-policy organization, but we share a responsibility to help tell the story, and sometimes that means sharing it in a policy arena or with government bodies.

**The Illinois Food, Farms, and Jobs Act**
Passed in the summer of 2009 by Illinois governor Pat Quinn, this new policy will direct government food purchasing toward supporting local farms and businesses as well as set in motion the planning of further initiatives to strengthen the economy of organic and sustainably grown food in Illinois. AOLC director Tom Spaulding was one of thirty-two members composing the task force created in 2007 to develop the plan, which responded to the revelation that 95 percent of the food consumed in the state comes from across state lines despite the fact that 80 percent of the land in the state is dedicated to agricultural use. This legislation sets the goal that by the year 2020, 20 percent of the food consumed in the state will be grown and processed locally— allowing for more of the nearly $48 billion the state spends on food to benefit the local economy. Visit Foodfarmsjobs.org for more information.

Opposite, top:
Thea Maria Carlson leads a group of medical students and teenagers around community gardens in the South Chicago neighborhood.

Opposite, bottom:
Martha Boyd outside the Chicago offices of AOLC. This demonstration garden is used for workshops with youth groups and community partners of the Urban Initiative division of the Learning Center.

When we think of a healthy local food system, we look at ecological sustainability: Is the land you are farming going to be healthy in twenty years or not? Are the rivers running cleaner than they were twenty years ago or not? Are people able to sustain themselves or their livelihoods better or not? These criteria must come into the conversation.

**How does the Urban Initiative approach residents?**
**TC**: There is a tendency to be imperialist when it comes to showing others how to do sustainable agriculture. We try to avoid that. Most of the people in the communities where we're working have been there much longer than us—we let them be in control of what happens there.

**Martha Boyd, Urban Initiative program director**: Every one of the Learning Center's initiatives is about building self-reliance, learning what people can do.

**Talk about one of your success stories.**
**TC**: We worked with both the Marjorie Kovler Center, a treatment place for survivors of torture, and the Chicago Waldorf School on a shared garden that was on land temporarily borrowed from Loyola University–Chicago. Even though those two groups were the ones managing the garden, other people in the neighborhood helped or dropped off food scraps for compost. Then Loyola said [it needed the land back]—the plan all along. The [people at the center and the school] felt paralyzed about losing the garden. We began to [strategize] how to reach out to all the wonderful people in the community and tell the story about how the garden positively affected folks.

At some point, a rumor developed that Loyola wasn't going to build on that land after all. All of a sudden people were saying, "Save the Sofia Garden!" And so we had this big community meeting of fifty people upset about how nothing was being done to save the garden. We explained about all of the work that had been done, about how we were documenting everything, and our plan for bringing more people in. Out of that meeting, people decided that the new space should be more of a community garden open to individual plot holders. We met with everyone, from the park advisory council to people down the street. In the end, thirty-two families were able to have plots in the garden, in addition to plots for community organizations.

**TS**: One of the best memories I have from the early years of starting the Learning Center on the farm was having the refugees from the Kovler Center out on the farm. The bridging of worlds—rural and urban, different nationalities, farmers and

**Farmer Training Initiative**
AOLC's training programs through the Farmer Training Initiative are in two parts: First is "Stateline Farm Beginnings," which is essentially a farm business-planning 101 course, with an emphasis on "whole farm planning," that aspiring farmers take at the Learning Center. The course was adapted from the work of Land Stewardship Project in Minnesota. The second half of the program involves a series of field days on various farms and working with a mentor farm from the Collaborative Regional Alliance for Farmer Training (CRAFT) farmer network, adapted from a program launched in New York state in 1994. This farmer-led coalition offers farmer-to-farmer training to the next generation of farmers. Between the relatively new farmers who have graduated from their Stateline Farm Beginnings course and those, both new and experienced, who have membership in CRAFT, the Learning Center has touched hundreds of small farmers throughout the region.

Pages 66–67:
Goats play an important part in the Learning Center's work, with many of their On-Farm Initiative training programs centered around goats'-milk cheese and soap. The soap is sold as a fundraiser for the organization.

nonfarmers, et cetera—and finding commonality, finding things to work on together, creates some interesting space for some miraculous healing to occur. Not just for them, but for us.

**Who are the people coming through your farmer training courses?**
**Sheri Doyel, Farmer Training Initiative program director**: Surprisingly, many people aren't from a farming background. More than 50 percent of our students are city or suburban people. Some have financial stability and want to change their lifestyle, live rurally. Some are looking to live closer to the land, grow their own food, and provide food for other people. Most are college-educated and are interested in systems—for example, the system of the farm, or the system of sales. They tend to be people who are not small thinkers; they tend to have a really good handle on the bigger picture. We are mainly training people to become entrepreneurs. And that takes risk, so it requires a certain maturity. Their learning curve and their willingness to dive into something that is different are astounding on so many levels. There is a lot of idealism in the room.

**What are some of the obstacles that stand in the way of starting a small, sustainable farm?**
**SD**: We identify four obstacles. The first one is huge: land access. Not necessarily ownership of but access to a city lot or a piece of land. The second is financing. We have a few students with resources, but most come without land or a big bank account. They have to be creative about financing and educated about getting loans. Next is market development. Most people know about farmers' markets, CSAs, or selling to restaurants—but not a lot of people know how to diversify so that they have financial stability or how to expand and shift to wholesale. And the last obstacle is lack of access to training and education. We offer farm business planning, and we partner with Michael Fields Agricultural Institute for their production workshops. Our CRAFT network provides mentorship and training in an informal way.

We are almost finished with a handbook on how to replicate our advanced farmer training components and CRAFT. It's a big part of our mission to help people replicate what we do.

**Farmers teach most of your workshops. What do you say when people ask about training the competition?**
**SD**: First, I say that we don't need to worry about that because the demand for locally produced food is so high. But at AOLC it is not uncommon for the first response to that question to be about demand and the second response to be

something about the benefits of generosity. There is almost something karmically motivating about helping people learn how to farm.

When we talk about how to define "success" we ask our students: Is it because 80 percent of your household income comes from the farm? Because the farm pays for itself? Is it because you have a sense of contentedness at the end of the day? How do you prioritize those things? We help people have a viable farm business in which they are farming sustainably.

**Where would you like to see the Learning Center in five years?**
**SD**: If more people take Farm Dreams, our half-day workshop, that is helping participants understand if they really want to get started farming. Tom says if 90 percent of the people who participate in Farm Dreams decide they are *not* going to farm, then it's been a success. Because this is not whimsical. It's a serious venture that could eat up all your resources if you don't do it properly or have the support. If more people explore what it takes to farm and have that permeate them, that will influence their buying habits, how they visit markets, or talk to their friends about food production. If the consumer base shifts, a huge amount of change is going to take place—and this would produce more sustainable farmers.

**TS**: During the next five years and into the next thirty we see continuing to ramp up the farmer training—passing on the skills and techniques of the current generation of **biodynamic** and organic growers in our region to the next generation who want to initiate farming. And we see expansion in the urban areas, working with more youth and more adults, broadening the work we are doing with those communities.

We are grounded in a **biodynamic** farm, and we see the farm as a living organism moving by 2030 into having a greater balance and more livestock to equate the vegetable production. In the next twenty years, I think you'll see us work together with Angelic Organics Farm to bring a dairy back and to reintroduce grains. And if there is grain production, then a bakery could be developed as well as additional value-added production to complement the vegetable production.

And with the On-Farm Initiatives, within the next five years we will build an overnight residential facility. This would be a place where groups from the city can come and stay for a week or longer—an ecological and beautiful space where they can be together in a temporary community while encountering the farm in its fullness. We are hoping that will be ready by 2013.

Opposite, clockwise from top left:
Angelic Organics runs one of the largest CSA farms in the country. Growing manager Bob Bower updates the planting and harvesting schedule with a fine-tipped pen.

Neighborhood gardeners in South Chicago prepare a vacant lot for a new garden.

Workshop attendees shake mulberry trees and gather the berries to press for wine.

Executive director of the Learning Center, Tom Spaulding participates in a wine making workshop.

Urban Initiatives Program Coordinator Thea Maria Carlson visits next to her car with Gregory Bratton of Healthy Southeast Chicago, a community partner starting a new urban farm. The Learning Center helps groups like this with their planning and development.

# THE SCIENCE OF PLANTS

# Native Seeds/SEARCH

Location:
**Patagonia and Tucson, Arizona**

Organizing body:
**20 staff, plus board members**

Scale:
**60 acres, plus retail store, seed bank, and three offices**

Type:
**Nonprofit**

Currently producing:
**O'odham pink bean, Taos red bean, Hopi red and Pima gray limas, Four Corner's runner bean, Tohono O'odham cowpea, Santa Domingo melon, yellow-meated watermelon, O'odham chiltepin, Chimayo and Cochiti chiles, O'odham peas, Hopi red dye amaranth, Zuni tomatillo, Taos blue corn, Early Baart and Sonoran white wheats, and Hopi and Tarahumara sunflowers**

In operation:
**Since 1983**

Web site:
**nativeseeds.org**

In the hundred-degree heat, the brown tepary bean's leaves will fold up so that they're shading each other and preventing water loss through the leaves' surfaces. It is a quality that enabled this early crop to survive. Traits like this were appreciated and encouraged by native farmers who have always known drought, the scorching heat, and soils baked hard by the unrelenting sun of the deserts of the American Southwest and northwestern Mexico.

The role of Native Seeds/SEARCH (Southwestern Endangered Aridland Resource Clearing House) is to conserve, distribute, and document varieties of agricultural seeds and wild relatives that have been a heritage of the traditional cultures in this region. The work is done to serve the local ecology, but it also contrasts the work of industrial plant breeders racing to craft new seeds that can withstand the heat waves and diseases of a warmer planet. At a time when the Svalvard Global Seed Vault in Norway is being constructed and national seed banks are at the mercy of war and civil unrest, Native Seeds is an essential player in the preservation and distribution of not only the seeds but the information within them. Some are the same varieties of maize, beans, and sunflowers cultivated here long before the arrival of Columbus. They still thrive when they are offered to the soil.

# Interview with Suzanne Nelson

**What land areas and crops make up Native Seeds?**

**Suzanne Nelson, conservation director**: Our area of focus in terms of conserving **agrobiodiversity** is the southwestern United States and northwestern Mexico—specifically, the area that lies between Las Vegas, Nevada, in the west and Las Vegas, New Mexico, to the east and between Durango, Colorado, in the north to Durango, Mexico, in the south. This area is characterized as "arid"—experiencing high temperatures and low, bimodally distributed rainfall that comes as summer monsoons and winter storms from October to January. Soils are typically low in organic matter and nitrogen.

More than thirty Native American nations or tribes are located in this broad region, though most indigenous communities in Mexico lack official recognition as sovereign nations. We provide free seed to Native American communities and individuals who live within our area of focus as a way of returning benefits for their contributions to the development and maintenance of **agrobiodiversity**. Our primary focus is seed banking—conserving them and getting them back out to be grown—but there is a really strong connection to the people part of the picture.

The crops have some fairly unique adaptations to harsh environmental conditions, and so there is a very real genetic component to our work in terms of conserving genes—because of the crops' potential use in other places and because [they honor a cultural heritage]. The cultures that utilize these crops in these harsh environments were really the stewards and developers of a lot of these genetic traits. The crops are integral to their foods and ceremonies, so there is also a cultural adaptation that is being conserved simply by preserving the physical entity of the seed—if you can grow the crop, then you can continue to sing the songs to bring the rain.

We have examples—about 1,800 individual collections—of domesticated crops, and their wild crop relatives, from traditional and Native communities in Arizona and New Mexico and from the Mexican states of Chihuahua, Sonora, and Sinaloa. These are also the places where our community work occurs—we have a long-running program in the Sierra Madre in Chihuahua, for example. Seed samples are maintained under frozen storage conditions at our office/"lab" in Tucson. Periodically these samples are removed from the freezers and grown out at our Conservation Farm in Patagonia, Arizona.

Opposite, top:
(From left) Chris Schmidt, Alex Sando, Suzanne Nelson, Lindsay Werth, and Chris Lowen.

Opposite, bottom left:
An overview of freezers at the conservation lab.

Opposite, bottom right:
Lindsay Werth hand pollinates squash, a time-consuming job. It takes five to seven males to pollinate one female.

We're just about to begin construction of a new 6,600-square-foot "conservation center" at Brandi Fenton Memorial Park, a local county park. The new facility will include office space, a 600-square-foot walk-in cold room, a 150-square-foot walk-in freezer, and a 1,000-square-foot "lab" for seed processing. We expect to be moving from our current office, which is in a crumbling adobe house and garage built in the 1930s, sometime in late spring of 2010!

**What is your personal connection to the Native Seeds project?**
I am a collector from way back. I started as a kid collecting pieces of broken glass. I love visual diversity. We have a seed vault—a big walk-in cold room—where all of our seeds are stored in glass or plastic see-through jars. There is shelf upon shelf of variation: color, size, shape, texture. I just love this visual and surface diversity, but under this is the genetic diversity. All of the differences in color, size, shape, and texture are the result of differences in genetic make-up. But for me it is really the connection: What's important is the fact that people grow them, that people have subsisted on them or relied on their differences for thousands of years—and are still doing that. It's that nexus between biological and cultural diversity that still gets me excited.

What does this mean for a farmer in the Sierra Madre? It means that they can feed their family more or provide a wider diversity of food, so that maybe they will get certain vitamins or minerals that they are not getting if they just plant the same one thing over and over.

I first came to Native Seeds in 1994 as a consultant to one of the projects that I now oversee in the Sierra Madre. In '95, I became permanent staff. The Treasures of the Sierra Madre project focuses on community development, potable water systems, gardening, orchards, and roof-top rainwater harvesting systems.

**What's the economy of your work? Do you sell seeds?**
Our three main sources of revenue include sales, memberships and donations, and grants. We are a nonprofit, so the local economy can have a big impact on what we are doing.

Seeds are made available to interested users—gardeners and farmers—through our mail-order catalog and Web site. We also provide seed at no cost to Native American communities and individuals living within the southwestern United States and northwestern Mexico.

**National Heritage Area**
National Heritage Areas differ from national parks and other types of federal designations because they do not impose federal zoning or regulations on land use and do not involve land acquisitions. Because a National Heritage Area is locally initiated and managed, it is a community-based conservation strategy that recognizes that the people who live in a heritage area are qualified to preserve its resources.

Through annual congressional appropriations administered by local national park unit partners, up to $10 million in 50 percent match funding is available to each National Heritage Area during a period of fifteen years. This seed money helps cover basic expenses, such as staffing, and also leverages money from state, local, and private sources to implement locally selected projects.

Opposite, top left:
Chris Lowen sorts sunflower seeds.

Opposite, top right:
Benito Gutierrez with wheat.

Opposite, bottom:
Sunflower shelter/pollination control.

## How is your work coordinated with other initiatives?

We do a lot of partnering with groups in the area and in Mexico. We are just one part of a much larger picture. We don't go onto a reservation and initiate projects, but we can supply a really critical element. Most efforts are food related: seed sovereignty, food security, et cetera. The communities in this region are all very agriculturally based, so their cultural integrity largely depends on their agricultural integrity, which of course depends on access to seeds. We partner with the Community Food Bank, Native American groups, and others whom we provide workshops to. But we don't initiate these relationships; rather, we support local efforts that find their way to us.

We are part of an initiative called the Santa Cruz Valley National Heritage Area Act that aims to create a 3,300-square-mile heritage area, like a food shed, in the Santa Cruz Valley bordering Mexico.

## What are your biggest challenges?

Cross pollination. Depending on the crop, we use a variety of techniques to prevent pollination between different varieties, from putting them in a cage—in which insects can't get in or out so their pollen can't be crossed—to doing all hand pollination. Growing crops for seeds is a slightly different thing than growing them for eating. It is interesting to see people come to the farm, especially volunteers. They have this vision of coming down to this idyllic farm with all this great food. We do have great food, but we mostly need the seed, so you can't eat the ears of sweet corn.

## How can your work be integrated into larger social or ecological systems?

When we have large crops of squash, but we only need the seeds, we provide the rest of the fruit to a food bank or soup kitchen. We do try to make use of our waste, but a lot of our waste is essentially compost.

We would like to branch out, but we've tried that and failed, for example with integrating animals on the farm. When resources are limited you need to stay focused on your main task. So that is what we have been trying to do: focusing on our real mission of making sure that the seeds we are stewarding remain viable and that we can get them back out and promote them through a whole host of different venues.

Opposite:
Volunteer Ashlie West
packages heritage lentils.

**Seed bank**
A seed bank stores seeds as a source for planting in case seed reserves elsewhere are destroyed. It is a type of gene bank. The seeds stored may be food crops or those of rare species reserved to protect biodiversity.

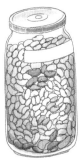

### Where would you like Native Seeds to be in five years?

I would like to see two things: first, a move in a direction that involves looking at our region as an entity that shares environmental and cultural similarities. In terms of issues related to food security and sovereignty, that means really taking a regional approach both at local and governmental levels as well as tribal and nontribal. That means looking at this as a participatory thing whereby everyone who lives in this region has a stake in this.

Second, more work in the field with small-scale farmers. Rather than just focusing on a "seed bank" type of operation, whereby seeds are essentially held in suspended animation, we would work to preserve the processes that are what created that diversity. For instance, farmer-participatory breeding—moving things back into the field and letting farmers grow their own seed. And if a particular race is not something that farmers are interested in anymore, that is okay, because they are evolving a new race—their selection over generations is going to result in the evolution of a new race or variety that is of more interest to them or is better adapted to growing conditions today rather than fifty years ago.

# Mountain Gardens

Location:
**Burnsville, North Carolina**

Organizing body:
**1 staff, 1 full-time resident, and up to 6 apprentices**

Scale:
**2.8 acres and on-site pharmacy**

Type:
**For profit**

Currently producing:
**Chinese and Appalachian medicinal herbs**

In operation:
**Since mid-1970s**

Web site:
**mountaingardensherbs.com**

In the mid-1970s, Joe Hollis left the city of Detroit for a life at the foot of Mt. Mitchell in the Appalachian Mountains of North Carolina. He wanted to break free of the economy and politics that he thought promoted war and oppression in favor of a life that would build on Gandhi's principal of "being the change you want to see." The change he wanted was minimal money economy, less harm to the earth, and egalitarian human relations. For the last three decades he has sought to live out his theory of "Paradise Gardening," joined by a rotating cast of natural builders, medicinal herbalists, family members, and interns. Inspired by his time in Borneo serving in the Peace Corps and his dedicated reading of philosophy, religion, anthropology, and plant science, Hollis has always sought to put ideas into action.

Mountain Gardens has one of the largest collections of Appalachian and Chinese medicinal herbs in the country. The Mountain Gardens land itself serves as an incubator for a wide variety of projects, from herbs to medicines to natural-building experiments. The most impressive part is the patience displayed there, with the first many years serving as a period for clearing land, sorting out the available resources, and considering possible futures. His many visitors can observe that almost everything is placed meticulously and comes from the land itself. Mountain Gardens is an example of an immersive, life-long practice rooted in a place and a self-made philosophy.

Top:
The central facility of Mountain Gardens is built primarily with lumber from the land on which it sits. Much of the space at Mountain Gardens is divided into distinct zones that connect through a complex web of trails and staircases, reflecting some of the tendencies encouraged through perma-culture, a natural-systems approach to agriculture.

Bottom, left:
The herb-formula tinctures are sold to visitors with a diagnosis from a practitioner of Chinese Traditional Medicine. The tinctures are made from organically grown herbs or from native plants in the area.

Bottom, right:
Mountain Gardens is more like a botanical garden or library of plants than a traditional garden, with labeled plants at different stages of development through-out the grounds.

# Interview with Joe Hollis

**Describe the southern Appalachian region.**
**Joe Hollis, founder**: Well, ecologically, they're very old mountains. Oldest on the continent, probably. Mt. Mitchell, the highest mountain in the east, is one of the more biodiverse areas of the southern Appalachians because there's a mixture of southern and northern floras. Because of the glaciers, plants moved south along the mountains and then moved back north as the southern things moved up. They mingled here. A lot of the plants that grow here are related to the plants that grow in eastern Asia. They are sister **bioregions**, or what's called a "botanical disjunction."

There's also topographic diversity and different plant communities. It has mostly to do with elevation, moisture, and pH variants. There's a long heritage of collecting and gathering medicinal herbs around here.

**How did Mountain Gardens begin?**
My intention was to try to develop a lifestyle that would present a solution to all sorts of problems. Which comes down to a) preventing ecological destruction, b) peace and justice, and c) what I consider indispensable, personal happiness. I had the idea that I would spend my life doing one project, so I wanted it to be as perfect a project as I could come up with. I spent some time thinking about how. . . . Because I wanted to develop a lifestyle that would be as widely applicable as possible, I knew I would have to grow food.

I'd go down to Chapel Hill in the winter for a couple months and bury myself in the library. I read about ecology, about ways people lived all around the world at different times, about civilizations, anarchy, gardening techniques. I read about sustainability, looking for unusual forms of agriculture that seemed more permanent, stable, tree crops, that kind of stuff. A lot of it was like anthropology. At some point, it just jelled: The difference was, either you are living as part of civilization—the State or the Economy—or you're living as part of the natural system. There's a big divide.

During the long hours I was making the garden, I was thinking about how to integrate new information and ways of thinking about the plant world. I considered a certain amount of politics and principles having to do with hand labor, using strictly the materials that were here, stuff like that. After seven or eight years, I had a pretty clear idea of what I was trying to do.

Above:
Joe Hollis tends to some
young plants in the area
beneath the main building.

**What were some of your early projects?**

The first spring I was here, I learned how to build a log cabin. I didn't know any-thing about it. It took a couple of years to build.

For about five years I just worked on making garden beds. When I started off, I'd clear little areas and sort rocks for steps, flagstones, walls, gravel paths. A friend had a gravely tractor, like a rototiller but more powerful. He went 'round and 'round, just hitting huge rocks. It was ridiculous—[the land] was about 70 percent rock all the way through. That's about the only time there's been a machine on this property. A lot of the terraces down through the vegetable garden got made in the first five or six years.

**At what point did you start doing things with medicinal herbs?**

At first I put myself in the landscaping business. I already had a lot of flower gardens: colorful English flower gardens, perennial borders, et cetera, which was relatively unknown in this country, certainly in this area at that point in time. I had this place planted up with plants to use for putting in gardens for other people.

Then at some point I realized that I was spending too much time away from home, and too much of my energy was going into gardening for other people. So my garden shifted from growing plants I could use for the landscape business back to the original concept of growing useful plants. The idea of a paradise garden began to shape up: It would be beautiful and the sum total of all the plants would be enough to live on.

In the course of that shift, I turned my focus to compiling a database—this was before computers—of the "thousand most useful plants," a project that has been ongoing. I went through maybe fifty different books about useful plants, ranging from the *Dictionary of Economic Plants* and *The Encyclopedia of Edible Plants of North America* to the *Medicinal Plants of the Cherokee Indians* to the *Wild Edible Vegetables of Northern Japan*. I had already worked out the **bioclimatology** of this area and matched it to similar areas, so that the plants that people use elsewhere could be naturalized here. Again, that was part of the concept—to have the plants be naturalized so that you're not constantly working against nature to keep them alive.

I assigned a reference number or letter to each plant that was mentioned in each book. I used green if it was in reference to its edibility, red if it was in reference to its medicinal properties, or black if it was for some other use, like craft, fiber, paper, basketry, et cetera. Certain plants would just jump off the page, like chickweed, which has about thirty references. Eventually I'd like to print a guidebook that would tell you what you're looking at when you walk through the gardens here. Every plant has a story.

**Is there one iconic plant that's most associated with Mountain Gardens?**
The plant that a lot of people would probably associate with me, the plant I promote fairly enthusiastically and sell the most of, is called Gynostemma pentaphyllum, or Southern ginseng, immortality herb, magic grass, or sweet tea vine, even though it actually tends to be bitter. It's got a lot of the same properties and compounds as ginseng, just more of them. You don't have to dig it up, and it grows like a weed. You harvest it aboveground, and then you can dry it in a day or two, and you can make a tea out of it. In every respect, it's a lot easier than ginseng. It has **adaptogenic** properties—it's good for immune systems, it's being used a lot for cancer prevention, blood-pressure regulation, cholesterol regulation, weight loss, and stamina.

**What are some of your current projects?**
I'm part of the Medicinal Herb Consortium, a nationwide group of growers who are the first generation of people in this country trying to grow Chinese herbs. The whole concept is about fifteen years old. I'm also part of an alternative agriculture working group seeking to develop Chinese herbs as alternative crops to tobacco in this area. I grow the plants and have the propagating material. We have way more buyers than we have growers. So we're looking to set up about ten test plots around the western part of the state.

Opposite, top:
Steve Barineau is the only other current permanent resident of Mountain Gardens besides Hollis. Steve specializes in natural building and helps to maintain the grounds. The entire place is pretty informal, and no strict work schedule is maintained. Most people who stay for a long period do some combination of their own projects and general work to keep the gardens going.

Opposite, bottom right:
Wasabi.

Opposite, bottom left:
Southern ginseng.

At the same time, I have this project going with oriental perennial vegetables and native wild foods. I'm really interested in perennial food plants. You don't have to disturb the ground every year. I've been growing some of these perennials for twenty-five years and nobody ever asked for them. Suddenly, I am getting a lot of interest in these things, which is great.

I'm going to set out little areas of the garden for things like Indian cucumber root, which is a delicious little tidbit, but usually too small to be economically practical. So I'll just work with it. There's another one called Giant Solomon's Seal. There's a half-dozen native food plants that I'm experimenting with cultivating in a way that does not disturb the ecosystem, such as the local wild food plant called "ramp."

**What is the economy of Mountain Gardens?**
If I [could] make money by figuring out how to grow these wild food plants and perennial vegetables in a more intensive fashion, that'd be more productive. I still don't produce nearly all the food that I need to feed everyone who works here. As it is, I live on less than $8,000 a year. I stay below the poverty line. I really do spend all my money on my garden.

**What is the range of things that are currently for sale?**
Primarily plants. And also seeds and tinctures. A lot of those are made from things that are harvested off the land. Hopefully there will be more in the future—with more people, more can be harvested off the land and turned into a **value-added product**. I'm not into selling produce; I'm into selling **value-added products**. My money comes increasingly from teaching, selling to restaurants, and also from prescriptions down at the herb shop.

**Your philosophy includes a belief in a democratic principle, that paradise gardening is something that should be available to all people. Can you talk a bit more about that principle?**
"Democratic" to me means making a positive value of living within our share of resources. As long as you have an unequal distribution of wealth, you will have war, people trying to dominate other people. So it's a matter of setting up an entirely different value system. And that's where this dichotomy comes in of living on Earth versus living in civilization.

A conclusion I reached in the course of my reading is that consumption is basically communication. Once you get beyond basic human needs, we are consuming to make a statement about who we are by where we live, what we wear, where

we go on vacation, what we do for entertainment. That's not part of being human,
that's part of being civilized. If you get back to being human, you have a lot of
hunter-gatherers who absolutely wanted to have the minimum amount of stuff
because they had to carry it around with them. There is a value system in having
as few possessions as possible, to know how to make your living from where you
are, throwing together a shelter or whatever.

**Working in this way seems to require that people come out and visit. How do
you outreach to others and promote your ideas?**
I do a lot now through the Internet that I could never do before. And I try to get as
many people out here as I can on farm tours. If I really was successful at [doing
outreach and promoting], I'd never get anything else done. There's no doubt a fine
line with it.

I read an essay a long time ago that influenced me a lot: "The evening with Mon-
sieur Teste" by Paul Valéry. The gist of it is that by virtue of the fact that somebody
is known, or makes themselves known to you, they are that much less than this
theoretically perfect genius you never heard of. There are these theoretically
perfect geniuses out there, whom you've never heard of, because they are so
theoretically perfect and self-contained that they don't do any outreach whatsoever.
And they're almost invisible. That idea always stuck with me.

I could just do 100 percent my paradise garden, and it would be better than it is.
On the other hand, the whole point for me is the outreach, to try to influence
people. There is always that back-and-forth.

**Where would you like to see Mountain Gardens in five years?**
The fact is, I've got too many irons in the fire. My eyes are bigger than my stomach.
I feel like they're all good, interesting projects, and there should be people out
there interested in doing them. I've got the beginnings here, and I'm just looking
for people who want to take it up and really see where they can go with it.

# THE LOCALIST ENTREPRENEURS

# AquaRanch

Location:
**Flanagan, Illinois**

Organizing body:
**1 boss, 2 full-time staff, and
1 to 3 part-time staff**

Scale:
**Twelve 1,200-gallon tanks and
a 12,500-square-foot greenhouse**

Type:
**For profit**

Currently producing:
**Tilapia fillets; basil vinaigrette;
lettuce; Genovese, cinnamon, red,
and lemon basil; chard; spearmint;
tomatoes; and jalapeño, cayenne,
Anaheim, and bell peppers**

In operation:
**Since 1985**

Web site:
**aquaranch.com**

Myles Harston is an inventor. After spending years working in commercial plastics used in the agricultural industry, in the mid-1980s he began to experiment with aquaculture (fish farming). He discovered the work of Dr. James Rakocy, at the University of the Virgin Islands, who was focusing on developing new approaches to recirculating water systems that would combine raising fish with hydroponics (growing plants without soil, using only water and nutrients). The result is aquaponics. The fish excrete waste into the water, which is converted by bacteria into nitrates. The plants consume the nitrates from the water.

These systems can grow many varieties of plants, but trellised tomatoes and leafy vegetables work best on Harston's system. There is an economic advantage to having the fish and plant combination: The sale of either can subsidize losses for the other. In Harston's case, it is his herb crops, and his wife's famous basil vinaigrette salad dressing—made with basil grown in the fish-water aquaponics systems—that sells the best.

# Interview with Myles Harston

**How did you get into fish?**

**Myles Harston, founder**: As a kid I always had aquariums around the house. My mother used to take the fish water and water her plants. That fish water was good for plants and that led me to aquaponics.

**Were you involved in other kinds of agriculture before aquaculture?**

I was involved in making plastics for the agriculture industry, making grain storage. And I still do that, make equipment for the aquaculture industry. Plastics and fish go well together. The right kind of plastics are not hazardous to fish or people, and they don't deteriorate. So I make these tanks and filtration systems from scratch. I get the metals and weld them myself. The stuff I make is generally better than the high-tech stuff because it uses no energy to run. But it does the job.

When I first started working in the aquaculture industry in '85, I went around to a lot of different universities and started asking questions. It was amazing that I could ask the same question about indoor recirculating systems of six different [professors], and I could get six totally different answers. That left me with a lot of frustration. There were a lot of people with PhDs but without any real-world experience.

**Do you think not having a blueprint allowed you room for experimentation?**

Yes, it became an advantage. The clarifier I first developed worked really well. I described what I had done to some professors—and they said there was no way it would work, since it didn't use electricity. I finally had a guy come out and look at it. He still said it was impossible. He silently watched while I turned the valves on and off. Then he said, "Well it obviously works, though I can't explain how it works." Since then, everyone that has used our system says it's the most efficient system—especially for the price.

**How does the recirculating system work?**

The water sits in tanks. Then it moves to the clarifier, which separates out the particulates. The water moves from that unit to the ends of the grow beds. Then the water goes through the grow beds. There are about ten inches of water in the grow beds. There are floats on top of the grow beds, and plants are planted in holes in these floats. The plant roots are able to reach down into the water and get all the nutrients they need. The plants create a high amount of surface area, which is needed for beneficial bacteria. That helps to break down the ammonia so it's not

Top:
Myles Harston works in his
central Illinois facility. He regularly discusses the potential
for this kind of operation to be
easily adapted to urban areas.

Bottom, left:
Plants are grown with
aquaponics, a system that
combines raising fish with
hydroponics.

Bottom, right:
Harston feeds the fish.

toxic to the fish. The roots take up nitrogen from the water and turn it into less-toxic nitrates. Then water goes around to a tank, is pumped into a biofilter, and then by gravity it is sent back into the fish tanks. The fish are grown in round tanks so that current can be maintained to stimulate the fish to swim against the current. This swimming activity creates a firm texture to the fish resembling that of fish in the wild.

**How do you deal with waste?**
In terms of the water, most of the waste stream is utilized by plants. In the summertime we are able to use it outside in compost. We don't have that capacity during the winter yet. Eventually we would like to have a greenhouse that could be just for the heavier water. We have a small sewer system in our community, and [our waste] actually helps that system because we have the chlorine removed. We also have a high microbial life, which stimulates the city sewers, which is a good thing. We prefer not to send it that direction but sometimes we have to.

We only lose about 1 percent of our total water per month, which is not very much. Especially when you consider that most recirculating aqua systems loose 20 to 25 percent of their water every day.

**What's the scale of the operation?**
About 30 percent of our business is fish, the other 70 percent is divided between produce and **value-added products**. We have the ability to produce about five hundred pounds of fish every two weeks.

**In policy and activist circles, people talk a lot about "food miles" to measure the distance that food travels. How does this relate to your work?**
Western Illinois University–Macomb says that the average distance that food travels to reach the consumer's plate in our state is 1,500 miles. That's because we get a lot of food from California and from Mexico. And that means whatever we do right here saves a lot of energy. It means we will have better quality. And a lot of food that is imported is poorly inspected or checked, so that's a concern as well.

Aquaponics makes great sense in an urban area, because you can pretty much set it up anywhere. I would be interested in being a part of a committee to try to interject what is practical and what's not, what's feasible and what's not. But I'm not a politician. I'm a country bumpkin and I would like to keep it that way.

Above:
Harston shows how the roots
hang in fish water.

My farm is only a greenhouse. We only have a little bit of acreage around it. What I do could be duplicated in the city, as long as we have an abandoned building and an empty parking lot. It can be done very efficiently.

I think that we can eventually supply a huge portion of the food needs for a community in a city like Chicago. Chicago is one of the largest inland consumers of fish in the nation. Yet most of the fish we consume around here comes from outside not only our state borders but our borders, period. That, to me, can be resolved right here.

**Where do you want to see things in five years?**
I would very much like to see communities be able to produce their own food locally. I would like to see people look more at the quality than the cheap price. People often go to the big-box stores to get food. When you buy cheap food with a lot of additives in it, you are simply not as healthy as when you buy food that is natural. There would be fewer people going to the emergency room and less reliance on pharmaceutical companies for drugs. People live longer these days but their quality of life has deteriorated.

# Wild Hive Farm, Café, and Bakery

Location:
**Clinton Corners, New York**

Organizing body:
**2 at café and bakery, 2 at farm**

Scale:
**Café and bakery, plus 400 acres**

Type:
**For profit**

Currently producing:
**Heritage wheat**

In operation:
**Since 1982**

Web site:
**wildhivefarm.com**

Wild Hive Farm is so called because Don Lewis started as a beekeeper in 1982, a skill he learned during two years spent in Israel as a young man. His honey business led him to sell Middle Eastern–style honey-based pastries at the Union Square Market in Manhattan throughout the 1980s. To distinguish his product in 1999, he began by including 10 percent locally grown grains. By 2006, he had moved to using 100-percent local grains, custom-grown at Lightning Tree Farm near Millbrook, New York, and at three more farms farther north. The surplus created an additional line of flours and processed grains for the home baker.

The bakery and café he runs was once the Clinton Corners general store. Lewis is famous for his mobile, wood-fired hearth oven that he takes to county fairs as a way to lure people into the magic of locally produced bread and butter. The mission is really about local economics. Lewis says, "The best way to ensure a stable future for our local farmers is to support them financially. Wild Hive Farm does this reliably, as we buy our grains and produce exclusively from local and regional farmers and refuse to make any substitutions with commodity-grown grains."

Opposite, top:
Overlooking Lightning Tree
Farm, near Millbrook, NY, where
Wild Hive grows their grain.

Opposite, bottom:
Instructions for cleaning grain.

# DIRECTIONS for GRAIN CLEANER - (TOP→BOTTOM)

SLOT #1 → Big Screen Size - (ex. Peas 24^RD) w/ solid cover to close
  → BALL SCREEN (3:2)  (Triticale ~~~) (SPELT 14 RD-METAL FRAME)
       RD 14  H.R. Wheat  S.W. Metal FRAME Size 14
       Wheat

SLOT #2 → Solid PLATE w/ SQUARE HOLES TOWARDS front

SLOT #3 → Smaller Screen Size - (ex. PEAS 12^RD) (5½ x 3/4 Slots) w/ open lip to close
       → wheat, spelt, Triticale
  → BALL SCREEN S.W. 1/14 x ½ SLOT

SLOT #4 → Solid METAL PLATE W/ OPEN SLOT NEAR FRONT

SLOT #5 → Smaller Screen Size - (ex. PEAS 12^RD) w/ solid cover to close
       SAME
  → BALL SCREEN          (5½ x 3/4 slots)
       S.W. 1/14 x ½      → wheat, spelt, triticale
       SLOT

CORN: 32,~~~  S.W.: ~~~ SLOT      1/16 X 2 - SLOT
  MY NEED 24-30  28  16 OR 14 RD                    OATS
                15RD
       TRITICALE 8¾, 1/14 x ½/2, 1/14 x ½
                         SLOT

BECARE
   ^S
     OF

   LOO

# Interview with Don Lewis

**Can you talk about the local farm culture? There seem to be many young and just-starting farmers in this valley.**

**Don Lewis, founder**: It's true. A lot of the older farmers here, their children, and the next generation missed it. This is a new generation coming up. My father was a farmer and I am a farmer, but my generation bailed. So there's a resurgence that's going on now.

**Has anything you've done had a direct or indirect effect on policy?**

This is my twenty-sixth year in the green market, farmers' market system in New York City. This project of reintroducing cereal grains for human consumption to be grown here after an eighty-year hiatus has developed during the last ten years. The first year about 8 percent of my flour was locally grown, the next year it was 12 percent, and I just kept upping every year. I made boards listing the ingredients, and I highlighted the organic local ingredients with an asterisk. I made that standard on my table and then put up a sign: "Our Local Ingredients and Our Suppliers"—but none of that was policy. The only policy you had to oblige was that if you had a packaged good it needed a New York state regulation. I took it a little further. I was ready to lose consumers [due to the higher cost of local, organic ingredients], but I was gambling that I would gain others. That's exactly what happened. There were different stages in making changes to my business in that manner, starting with educating my consumers about what's really happening, and then as it increased, I got a little more vocal. The farmers' market space was my soapbox.

After I did all that with my signage, the green market made it their policy that you had to list ingredients on a sign on the table and highlight local ingredients. Now they've put into the regulations that all bakers must use locally grown grains for their production. If that's difficult to do, you can write the director and get released from the responsibility. They have taken that step so that in the future all producers will use locally grown grain. So it's in the regulations because of the example that I set. It's a tremendous struggle for a bakery to switch from commodity ingredients to local ones because of the cost.

We do a lot of lectures on what we've done, on creating a certified kitchen, and how to pass along the price to consumers without a shock. It takes a long time to get a kitchen certified: You have to have a three-bay sink and keep it clean,

Opposite:
Don Lewis presents a hard, red winter wheat that he has been growing as a spring wheat. "It's about 30 percent larger than most grain . . . it has a beautiful flavor, and if you bite it you can see that it has a lot of moisture in it."

separate hand-washing sinks, and separate areas for cooling and cooking bread. Now that we have one, we can share it with the community. Other than that, my contribution is the constant education of consumers on what they eat and what I feel is important.

That fifty tons of grain grown here, milled, and sold by us is mostly done within forty miles, sometimes up to one hundred miles from here to New York City. Having the availability, or access, is the key thing. Providing access changes the community.

**What is the history of the wheat?**
It is a non-GMO modern wheat. It's not a **heritage grain**. It's a little short for me, though. We have since seeded many farms with the same variety. Now we're on a project test-growing **heritage grains** and hoping to reintroduce them to the Hudson Valley. To be considered "**heritage grain**," it must have been grown more than 125 years ago here in the northeast.

**Heritage grains** are extremely exciting to me. I represented the Hudson Valley as a delegate for **Slow Food** at the **Terra Madre** conference recently. While I was there I bought an old-variety corn that had been grown here. Corn is from the Americas first of all, but [this particular native variety was obtained] from here 100 years ago or more; these people I met had been coveting it and keeping it genetically pure all those years. I brought samples back to try to reintroduce it to the area. The other really exciting thing is the growing of emmer wheat that's happening here this year.

**That's the next grain you'll introduce?**
The emmer is exciting. It's ancient, it's the grain that Moses carried, it's the first wheat, long before hard red, long before spelt. This will be the second season that amaranth will be grown on this farm and in New York state, and it will be the first season it will be sold commercially. It has tremendous nutritional qualities, and there has been research that claims that some of the qualities in wheat that make people suffer from intolerance are not present in amaranth. So the thinking is that people with celiac disease will be able to eat amaranth.

**So the goal is to come up with a few varieties rather than one superwheat?**
A few varieties that are strong and grow well up here in the Northeast, taller than the weeds, that stand up and don't get knocked down, and have good flavor and nutritional value, because that's all been bred out. Modern wheat has been bred for mechanization.

Top:
Don Lewis and Amy Lawton
(a partner in Wild Hive Bakery)
work the counter surrounded
by Ethel's German Porcelain
garlic. "Gilroy's got nothin' on

us. I spent time out in Gilroy
[California] once. Even our
local Germantown Farm has
three thumbs up on Gilroy,"
explains Lawton from behind
the bushels of garlic.

Bottom, left:
Close up of wheat that made
Lewis so happy.

Bottom, right:
Wild Hive Café and Bakery in
Clinton Corners, New York.

## How could this be sustained without fuel?

When I was eighteen, I lived on a collective farm in Israel raising fish. I knew several old-timers who were probably in their late eighties whose job used to be harvesting wheat with a scythe. One guy could hardly walk—it would take him ten minutes to get across the room—but he had arms that were bigger than my legs. People have been harvesting wheat by hand for years, so as far as post-oil, anything is possible, especially if the movement to return to heritage varieties is successful, because the grains will be taller and more manageable. Back when they used to harvest by hand the quality was so much better. When the modern farmer picks with a combine, he waits until he has the highest volume of quality wheat per head, but all of it is not quality.

There are sacrifices. But when you pick wheat by hand, you gather it into shocks and dry it, you start harvesting it. If it rains you take it inside and finish drying it, and then you thrash it. So you are getting the highest quality wheat. Harvesting by hand gives you the option of picking wheat at its peak, and then finishing it—you end up with a much higher-quality food.

## What's the biggest challenge?

Cash flow and personality. I work hand-to-mouth and I have always done that. I've never had government support and I'm not endowed. We have a really great team. It takes a team because we have to work together and focus. I am taking on a partner who will help me facilitate and organize for my next phase, which is a good thing. There are grants available and organizations willing to help me find and apply for them, and there are donors out there. I'm looking forward to the support because I've always lived on the edge.

## Where do you see Wild Hive Farm, Café, and Bakery in five years?

I'm hoping to finish phase two of my operation, which is to move my mill and my chicken production into a new, larger space that can facilitate the public, so that school groups can come, see the mill run, and understand the concept. For years now I have been doing milling demonstrations at markets and festivals, and it's the children who are drawn to it like moths to a flame—that's where the emphasis has to be. They go straight to their parents with a handful of flour and dictate to them about what it is.

Above:
Electric grain dryer.

And I would like to move my grain cleaning [to the new space] so that I'll be able to do it rather than relying on folks here at the farm. Because this a certified-organic farm, I don't have the ability to bring noncertified grains to run through their equipment. Although I could be a certified mill and bakery, I choose not to be. In building the system, you need to have some diversity; if you lock into certified organic right away, it's not a level playing field. In other words, you're not opening up to new growers who want to grow grain for human consumption who are not certified organic. I'd rather give growers a chance to get into growing for human consumption using organic standards, but without the restrictions of organic certification. This way they can feed the community and get a better price for their product and then eventually, once they're up and running, they can become certified. We need to build the system and then sharpen it later.

**What's been the most joyous moment?**
I think it was reaching the point of making the bakery 100-percent heritage, because it hasn't been done and I wanted to make it happen.

# Georgia Citizens Coalition on Hunger

Location:
**Atlanta, Georgia**

Organizing body:
**5 staff, multiple volunteers**

Scale:
**2 acres**

Type:
**Nonprofit**

Currently producing:
**Collard greens, okra, and squash**

In operation:
**Since 1974**

Web site:
**Ga-hungercoalition.org**

The Georgia Citizens Coalition on Hunger (Hunger Coalition) began by doing community organizing and policy work related to urban poverty. In response to the lack of good food in the primarily African American neighborhoods they were working in, they started a farmers' market. Eventually they started growing their own food for sale at these markets.

Atlanta is a city at the center of a sprawling metropolitan region of more than five and a half million people. The city grew tremendously in the 1990s, partially due to massive investments resulting from hosting the 1996 Summer Olympics. The Olympics, always rife with controversy, were seen by many as an opportunity to rid the city of its poor population. Sandra Robertson, executive director of the Hunger Coalition, explains "That's when the homeless people disappeared. They were literally being given bus tickets out of the state. It was a rough and tough time, and people were in the streets protesting almost every day. Bulldozers were coming and knocking down major neighborhoods to clear way for the Olympics. Relationships were scattered, and people were dismantled, almost like in New Orleans, though not quite as dramatic, but in the same fashion."

This is the context in which an organization and a family has been built. This group of mostly women is undoubtedly family—in their ethos and approach to one another, to people seeking their services or looking to get involved. That loving attitude permeates their work and the atmosphere they have painstakingly created during the last thirty-five years. The most remarkable trait about their organization is a complete willingness to evolve if their ideas or mission need to go in another direction: first as an advocacy project, then an emergency-assistance hotline, then a food pantry and a support group, then a farmers' market and organizers of the annual Poor People's Day on the Georgia State Capitol's steps, then administrators of a social-justice community center, and now a farm.

# Interview with Sandra Robertson, Althea Morrow, Melissa Pittman, and Chris Edwards

**In the early years, the mid-1970s, Georgia Citizens Coalition on Hunger was mainly advocating for the creation and maintenance of programs like Women, Infants, and Children (WIC), farmers' markets, and school breakfast and lunch programs—programs to keep people from going hungry. In the '80s you worked around food stamps and then, as the welfare system was dismantled by Presidents Reagan, Bush Sr., and Clinton, the work changed. Why did you go from advocacy to more direct service and** direct action**?**
**Sandra Robertson, executive director**: It changed out of necessity. For instance, one day a woman called and said, "Do you all have any food? I have three children and I need food." I said, "We don't have food, but we have some powerful information, and we want to get you involved in helping us change the way the food stamp program is organized." She said, "Ma'am, I want some food. I don't want no conversation!" [laughter] I had a real awakening that day. We talked a lot with her. She gave us a real education about the economy, and we helped her get food and apply for food stamps so that she was able to stabilize her situation. This led to more conversations with the public, and it became clear that we needed some kind of program for emergency assistance.

We opened a hunger hotline in 1988. The first day of opening, we got ten or fifteen calls from people who needed help. Word got out and the number of calls started to grow. But our capacity was pretty small at that time. We only had enough food to sustain a person for a day or two. We could see that was not going to be enough. But we also had a number of conversations about how we didn't want to become a big pantry, that we wanted to have more than that. So we started to recruit people to work on issues around welfare, food stamps, social security—and so one thing led to another.

**What led the Hunger Coalition to start organizing farmers' markets in the early '90s?**
**SR**: At one point in our history, we had a buying **co-op** that purchased bulk food packages, including produce, meats, and staple goods. We could then offer people the opportunity to get relatively discounted prices on the food. That went really well for a while, but we wanted to try something else to encourage healthful eating and

**Women, Infants, and Children (WIC)**
Established in 1974, this program distributes food and nutritional services to pregnant mothers, infants, and children up to age five. It is facilitated by the Food and Nutrition Service (FNS) of the USDA. In most states the program provides vouchers that can be used in food stores, though the availability of all WIC services differs slightly according to state. The FNS is also the entity charged with coordinating programs such as food stamps, emergency assistance, and school breakfasts and lunches, which are all directly tied into the federally subsidized commodity food programs that are designed to control food prices.

These programs first came into existence during the Great Depression of the 1930s and have come under significant criticism by healthful-food advocates and domestic and international farmers alike for their encouragement of the overproduction of less-healthful plants such as corn and soy. Those and other "commodity" crops are either processed into nutritionally deficient food options or carelessly distributed to economically depressed regions of the world where local farmers are unable to compete with the free and subsidized food commodities from the United States (such practice is commonly referred to as "import dumping").

cheaper food packages—and that's when the farmers' market concept emerged. We started doing the farmers' markets in public-housing communities. We would set up the markets and the community would run them. We would issue $5 coupons to the community to introduce them to the concept of buying at a farmers' market. More people began to ask us to set up markets in their communities. We'd identify the farmers, and the people would develop relationships with the farmers.

After two or three years, I got a call from a man in Massachusetts who was trying to get a weekly **farmers' market coupon program** started in his state, but he was working at the federal level and wanted to get demonstration projects all over the country. He had heard that we were operating small farmers' markets, so he came down to talk to us about getting our state to apply for funding to have subsidized farmers' markets. We talked to the **Federation of Southern Cooperatives** and we appealed to the Department of Agriculture in our state. At first, they did not see a way that they could make that happen. But as time went on, they were convinced, and then somehow or another it ended up as part of the WIC program.

The first **farmers' market coupon program** became so popular that we expanded just about every year. We started operating some of them eventually because we ran out of farmers. And that's where we are today. We actually became farmers.

**How did the land that you farm and your Community Resource Center come about?**

**SR**: In the early 1990s we had a visioning session with a facilitator who was lent to us by the Community Foundation for Greater Atlanta. Fifteen mothers nervous about the cuts to the welfare system talked about wanting to have a way to control the prices of their food, wanting to have a garden or a farm where they could grow their own food. They talked about wanting to have a thrift shop. They described it like a mall where people could come and have all their needs met. They also talked about wanting to create jobs for themselves that paid at least $10 an hour [so that they could] run a large part of the project. That's how our building and farming land came about—because [our people inspired this visitor], and he in turn worked with the Foundation to help us get this place. It's a building in trust. We have a long-term lease for $1 a year.

**How did you go about preparing the land for growing food? What was your plan?**

**Althea Morrow, Umoja Garden manager**: I had been working in the thrift store starting in 2000, and I was fascinated by the garden, by farming, because in my childhood, I thought that I couldn't grow anything. We had a little experiment in kindergarten where every child grew a bean in a little cup. Mine was the only bean that didn't grow! So when Sandra asked me if I wanted to become the gardener, deep inside of me I was yearning for it, but I said, "I don't know how to garden!" Neither of us knew how to do anything!

**SR**: For two years or more, we had a pitiful harvest. We just kept working—we hadn't discovered that our ground wasn't healthy. Althea would tell me, this person says it needs this, or that person says it needs that, and we'd try it out, and then something green would show up, and we'd get excited. We would just learn as we went. A few years ago is when we started to actually grow something for someone to eat!

The Community Foundation for Greater Atlanta had a special Make-A-Wish grant that we applied for, and that's what got us the tractor. And that was great, because it really put us on another scale in terms of our capacity to till more ground and plant more vegetables.

**AM**: Each year, we would have a crop or two that would do real good, like okra or collard greens, and those would enter the farmers' market. What we can't sell or doesn't look pretty—it's an organic garden, so sometimes the bugs make the produce look a little funny—goes into the food pantry.

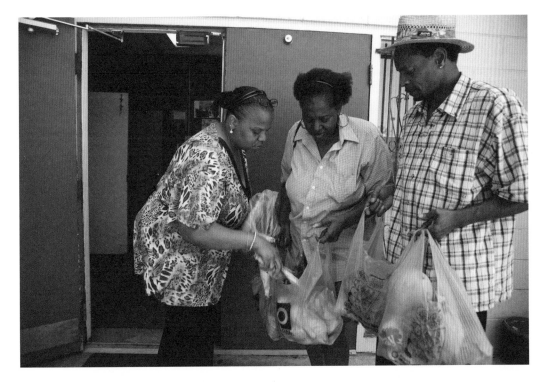

Top:
Carolyn Pittman adds fresh
corn to Vickie Swinger and
Clifford Pearson's produce
bags.

Bottom, left:
The Hunger Coalition—front
row: Melissa Pittman (center)
and Althea Morrow (left);
second row: Sandra Robertson
(center); third row: Carolyn
Pittman, La Tausha Nedd, and
Chris Edwards (from left);
back row: Mary A. Foster and
Anthony Barksdale (from left).

Bottom, right:
The Hunger Hotline has been
helping Atlanta residents since
1988. Mary A. Foster is on the
phone, with La Tausha Nedd in
the background.

**Your farmers' markets began in public housing in Atlanta in the mid-1990s. Where do you sell now and who are your customers?**

**Melissa Pittman, farmers' market manager**: When I first started doing the market, the farmers would come from southern Georgia, and we would go to maybe four housing projects; women in the housing projects would set up the tables for our fruits and vegetables. As the housing projects started to close, so did the market sites. So for a year or two, I think we might have had only one site, the Bowen Homes.

**SR**: After most public housing was torn down, people were spread all over the city and the sprawling suburbs of Atlanta. Now we do farmers' markets outside of WIC health clinics in the city and the suburbs.

**MP**: Now it's a completely different group of people. Because the other markets were more community-oriented, everybody knew everybody. The markets now serve people who live near the WIC center. And so they're far out from where we used to set up the markets.

**SR**: The people come for a specific service and a specific need. So there is a slightly different feel. We still try to keep it as festive as possible. But it's changed this year completely. We hardly see the customer anymore! The WIC program takes orders; they let the client fill out a little order sheet. So we don't know how it's going to feel in the end, but right now, we're not feeling excited about it—we really like the interaction with the customer, with the people.

**Could you imagine a policy initiative that would holistically address poverty in the way that you actually talk about in your mission to end poverty?**

**Chris Edwards, garden volunteer**: I think so. I see it as land ownership. If you can provide land to facilitate a way for people to take care of themselves, I think it's possible. If people got empowered by owning land, they might have the ideas: "I am going to grow my food. I don't have to pay for my health care anymore, I am my health care."

**SR**: I can envision us getting to a place where we are articulating broad, sweeping policy that could help transform the way we live together—and ensure everyone has a quality of life that is representative of a civilized society. There should not be any hungry or homeless people in America. It should be outlawed. It should be a crime to allow anyone in your city to go without shelter or food, because these

**Georgia Human Rights Union**

Unlike many organizations, the Georgia Citizens Coalition on Hunger coordinates its work on a legislative and street-protest level as well as through direct services. And unlike typical charity efforts, the group attempts to connect the act of giving food and relief with providing information and training, so that people can help themselves and organize their communities.

The wing of the organization that bridges this gap most clearly is the Georgia Human Rights Union, which is a hybrid of skill-sharing and political action. The group meets on a quarterly basis and draws mainly from the base of people who come to the Hunger Coalition seeking emergency assistance through the hunger hotline or the food pantry. Everyone is invited to come together and to discuss the deeper issues associated with poverty, from government negligence and policies needing reform to historical inequalities and unhealthy habits. They meet to help each other navigate the complexities of the welfare system and learn to cook healthful food from the garden.

Over lovingly prepared meals by assistant director Carolyn Pittman, the Union is a different approach to a self-help group, with a focus on community and cooperation.

Right, top:
Raejanne Lesperance (yellow shirt), "Maggie" Bassey (cap), Melissa Pittman (green shirt) and Briana Starks unload greens sourced from local farmers.

Right, bottom:
Althea Morrow and her daughter Barbara Mayo breathe out after a hot day in the garden.

[basic necessities] are the measure of a society that has reached a certain level of civility. I don't think there should be people without health care in our society, or without education. When we allow people to be ignorant, we all pay the price for it.

**Where would you all like to see the Hunger Coalition and its work in five years?**

**MP**: Well, our mission is to end hunger and homelessness in the state of Georgia, and in five years, with some magic, I'd like to see it ended! But realistically, I would hope that we have shared some education and knowledge about how to make this mission come to fruition at some point.

**SR**: We have another hub in Augusta, and we have an organizer there who is actually working with her church to try to use the property on the church land to have another garden, and to open up another hunger hotline. We'd love to see [this type of thing] spread to other places around the state.

# Nuestras Raíces

Location:
**Holyoke, Massachusetts**

Organizing body:
**27 staff (7 full-time adult staff, 5 part-time adult staff, and 15 paid youth staff), plus 14 college interns, hundreds of community volunteers from community gardens, youth groups, corporations, local churches, colleges, and probation departments**

Scale:
**10 community gardens, a 30-acre farm, and a café**

Type:
**Nonprofit**

Currently producing:
**Puerto Rican specialty crops like ají dulce (sweet pepper), calabaza, tomatoes, eggplants, sweet corn, and pigs, goats, rabbits, and chickens sold on the farm or for home slaughter**

In operation:
**Since 1992**

Web site:
**nuestras-raices.org**

Opposite, top:
Teens from the Nuestras Raíces Youth Program.

Opposite, bottom:
Market manager Jesus Espinosa keeps young customers happy with fresh picked blueberries at the downtown Holyoke farmers' market.

All of the work that Nuestras Raíces (Our Roots) does is related to food and agriculture in one way or another, but the real crux of its work is community and economic development in the small city of Holyoke, in western Massachusetts, populated primarily by U.S. citizens from Puerto Rico.

Nuestras Raíces was founded in 1992 by the members of La Finquita community garden in South Holyoke. The organization is now an incubator for ideas, projects, and small businesses. Some of the ambitious food-related practices include Tierra de Oportunidades, which launches small businesses on La Finca (The Farm). Another is the extensive network of more than ten community gardens throughout the city set up in schools and vacant lots.

La Finca houses a beginning farmer-training program that rents small plots of land, typically under an acre, to interested community members and provides them with small loans, training, shared resources, market assistance, and community support. The farm hosts four agricultural and food-based businesses: a farm store, a pig-roasting operation, a greenhouse, and a paso fino horse barn.

There are countless short- and long-term jobs, workshops, bushels of food, and fantastic weekly pig roasts that have been spawned through the work of Nuestras Raíces. As former industrial towns all over the country try to rethink their economies, deal with shrinking and unemployed populations, Nuestras Raíces is making sure that Holyoke and its residents are not like the rest of the statistics reflecting failed, dead, or hopeless situations.

# Interview with Daniel Ross, Ramiro Davaro-Comas, Jim Santiago, Julia Rivera, Raphael Rodriguez, and Tyrone Bowie Jr.

**Can you describe the context that Nuestras Raíces is operating in?**
**Daniel Ross, executive director**: Holyoke has been called the Paper City because it was once a center of the world's paper industry. Now, by most criteria, it's the poorest city in the Commonwealth and the sixth poorest city in the country: 28.6 percent of the households in the city earn less than $15,000 annually. Holyoke has the highest concentration of Puerto Ricans of any city—41 percent of the city's 39,000 residents—in the United States outside of Puerto Rico.

The Connecticut River Valley of western Massachusetts is a region with rich agricultural soils and heritage, first farmed by the Agawam and Algonquin Indians. Immigrants from Europe came in waves and settled in the valley and surrounding hills and established villages and farms. Today, agriculture in the valley is under extreme pressure from development, and farmers are aging, so the region is desperate for new farmers to take their place.

As our nation's demographics and agricultural economy change quickly, immigrants, refugees, and ethnic communities have become the movers and shakers of the food system—an estimated 78 percent of crop workers in the United States are foreign-born, according to the **USDA**'s Agricultural Resource Management Survey, and Hispanic farmers are the fastest-growing demographic group of new farmers in the country.

In addition to economic inequality, Holyoke's Latino residents suffer disproportionately from the health impacts of a dysfunctional food system, including such as high rates of hypertension, diabetes, asthma, and cardiovascular disease (CVD), according to Massachusetts Department of Public Health data. The prevalence of CVD in Holyoke Latinos is more than double the rate for Massachusetts residents. Holyoke public schools data indicates that more than 45 percent of children in the fourth grade are overweight or obese.

Opposite, top:
(From left) Sister Marie Thaddeus, SP, Sister Geraldine Noonan, SP, farmer Angel "Luis" Aponte, and Sister Elizabeth Oleksak, SP. The sisters' religious order, the Sisters of Providence, helped make a portion of La Finca land available to Nuestras Raices.

Opposite, bottom:
Recent immigrants from Turkey work the back acres of La Finca's perimeter.

**Ramiro Davaro-Comas, employee**: Access to healthful food is really hard for the people who live downtown. There's one place to go shopping there, a Costco, and it's all right. If you are on food stamps, you have to buy things that are twice as expensive.

A lot of businesses stopped coming here and stopped putting money into certain things. Building owners who didn't want to keep their businesses here, but couldn't move their things, started paying kids to light them on fire so that they could collect insurance money and leave. It happened a lot. There's one story about a woman who was killed inside a burning building. After that there was a huge movement here to stop it.

**DR**: When Nuestras Raíces started, people were already gardening here, but they wanted to continue and expand. Almost all the Nuestras Raíces members had backyard farms in Puerto Rico, with avocado, mango, and banana trees, as well as coffee. Many had worked in sugarcane fields and pineapple plantations. Many have lifetime experience in agriculture.

**Did Nuestras Raíces start with food and then eventually incorporate all these other related components, or did the organization begin knowing that they were intertwined?**
**DR**: We started with one community garden but we grew to respond to the needs and opportunities of the members. First the garden workers were all residents. Each new project and relationship grew from that first desire, along with the skills and culture of the members. We grew to include youth programs, farmer training programs, enterprises, and environmental education programs. It started with food, but that vehicle lent itself so well to understanding the heart of how to revitalize a community.

**How does food play into people's need for income?**
**Jim "Jimsan" Santiago, economic development director**: The gardeners grow their crops then go out and sell them or come to me [for advice on other options], like take them to restaurants, to the Farm Store, and to other ventures like bakeries.

I was talking to this kid recently about money, and he kept saying, "But the money's so quick; it's so quick," referring to drug money. And I told him that his life expectancy was real quick, too. The reason people sell drugs is because they don't have jobs, they don't have an income. They go that way because they need cash quick.

Above:
Julia Rivera chats with a neighbor in the community plots
behind their apartment building. The blue fencing reminds
her of Puerto Rico's gardens.

If we can open the eyes of the youth and get them to be entrepreneurs, it would
be a different story.

**How did the first community garden program start?**
**Julia Rivera, community gardens founder and organizing director**: I went to
the city council, then to the mayor, and told him about the big vacant lot near my
house that was in really bad condition, but that I wanted it for a garden. The city of
Holyoke cleaned the lot and put in more soil. We took kids ages seven to thirteen
there. The soil was so rich that the weeds grew so fast that we couldn't keep [the
plot] clean. The looks on their faces were great.

The first year we started with flowers. The next year the kids invited their parents to come. When their parents began to show up, we realized that we really could have a community garden. Nuestras Raíces provided everything—tools, seeds, everything. There are ten gardens now, and we are about to start another.

**Raphael "Rafi" Rodriguez, Youth Art and Food Systems group leader**: We have a blueberry patch, raspberry patch, and mulberry trees. Every once in a while the staff takes some to eat, but we sell most of our produce to try to raise money for a year-end activity or celebration. My family eats food from the garden because my mom has a plot; she brings up lettuce, cilantro, and tomatoes.

**In addition to the community gardens, there is also a farm. How did that get started?**
**DR**: It was just an incredibly lucky find. We now have thirty acres. We bought it all from a family that had owned it for four generations. Our understanding is that our farmland has been agricultural and cultural land going back to the Abalone Indians. We understand that it was a victory garden in World War I.

**Does the produce from the farm go to primarily farmers' markets or stores?**
**Tyrone Bowie Jr., youth coordinator**: There's a Farm Store here on the property. And then there are three farmers' markets that we sell to. We try to make connections with the local corner stores, but they are not happy with our rates or how quickly we can get the food out to them. They are only interested in what they can sell the fastest. If you go into the stores, you realize that the food's not worth buying.

**RR**: We started a salad bar at [William J. Dean] D-Tech High School to try to get kids into vegetables. Now we're starting another in the other [local] high school. The produce comes straight from here.

**DR**: The culinary students prepare the salads. Some of the kids work at the farms and have family members who work on the farm. We are building community food awareness, and we are cognizant that there aren't many places locally where this type of food is available except where we're doing it. We partner with Elder Services; they provide some of their **farmers' market coupons** to buy produce from our farmers, and they put together bags for homebound seniors of local, culturally relevant produce.

**Food and Fitness**
In 2006, the W. K. Kellogg Foundation announced funding for a new Food and Fitness Initiative that would create vibrant communities with easy access to locally grown, healthful, affordable food, as well as safe places for physical activity and play, for everyone.

Last year the Kellogg Foundation invited Nuestras Raíces to apply for the funding. Working with the Holyoke Health Center, the organization helped assemble a coalition of nearly seventy-five local groups that applied for a two-year planning grant. They were then invited to submit their ten-year plan for a chance to be awarded $3.75 million in funding. The coalition was one of just nine nationwide to win—a signal achievement for Nuestras Raíces and for the city. The coalition will use the funds to create a comprehensive plan for a unified, community-based system of access to healthful food and fitness opportunities, confronting the underlying poverty, blight, and social-justice problems within the community in the process.

Through facilitating collaboration across multiple sectors and generations, the goal is to develop integrated, sustainable, and practical solutions that will serve as models for other communities.

**The Pig Roast**

In keeping with Puerto Rican tradition, Nuestras Raíces holds a large, free pig roast every year. The event features a demonstration of paso fino horses, live *música típica de esencia tropical*, and, of course, traditional *lechón asado*, or Puerto Rican–style roasted pig. Vendors are charged a fee to help underwrite costs.

Pig roasts on a much smaller scale are held every Saturday on La Finca for $10 a person. The beautiful setting is a perfect place to bring the community together and be happy.

## Since the farm is an incubator for small businesses, are you doing money lending?

**DR**: We've had a grant from **Heifer Project International** for the past couple of years that allows us to loan money. Our beginning farmers have to go through a very intensive business training class in the winter. We assume that the twenty-five to thirty people who come to us at that point have some experience in farming and production, so we focus on business skills for doing commercial farming in Massachusetts: regulations, marketing, and financial record keeping. In eight weeks [students] put together a rudimentary business plan. The ones with the most viable plans, as assessed by a committee of established farmers and business experts, get the chance to have a plot at our incubator training farm, La Finca. At that point, they can apply for a micro-loan.

The loans are between $500 and $1,500, which covers seeds, start-up animals, everything. Since the Heifer funding is ending this year, we've established a relationship with a local financing agency called the Western Massachusetts Enterprise Fund that will allow us to extend micro-loans and larger loans as farmers expand.

## What's the biggest challenge for Nuestras Raíces?

**JR**: We need more community gardens, and we need to make sure that the city of Holyoke sets policies to provide community gardens for food, nutrition, and saving money.

**TB**: Our health problems wouldn't be so bad if we took a look at agriculture. To cut down the obesity problem in the United States, money could be put into agriculture, and we could build our youth program again. Our youth programs do so much. The youth are the ones that set up this land for everyone to work on. A few years ago we lost funding from the Ford Foundation, and we lost the program.

**DR**: Our challenge is helping Holyoke and other communities like it understand that urban agriculture and sustainable development are powerful in economic and community development. The model we are going for around the farm is that of agricultural tourism and cultural destination. Almost as a mall concept, we would have lots of different enterprises paying us rent and creating the traffic. We'd have licensing arranged with the Farm Store, the pig roast, the horse stable, and even the cultural events. One idea to make it sustainable would be to spin off the cultural events as an enterprise. We could run them as a business model.

# THE MARKET/CSA FARMS

# Freewheelin' Farm

Location:
**Davenport, California**

Organizing body:
**3 staff**

Scale:
**15 acres across
two plots**

Type:
**For profit**

Currently producing:
**Kale, onions, strawberries
and lettuces**

In Operation:
**Since 2002**

Web site:
**freewheelinfarm.com**

Located five miles north of Santa Cruz, California, one of Freewheelin' Farm's plots, at eight beautiful acres, supplies residents and businesses in the Central Coast community with fresh, organically grown fruits and vegetables. Since 2002, the farm has made it a policy to examine its resource consumption and conserve water in its irrigation practices. In pursuit of sustainability and its own ecological consciousness, Freewheelin' Farm works to decrease its petroleum consumption on all aspects of the farm: from reusing old drip tape year after year to building farm structures with reclaimed lumber, and, ultimately, as per its namesake, to delivering its Community Support Agriculture (**CSA**) shares by bicycle and trailer—a modern equivalent of the horse and buggy.

Beyond simply growing fresh, healthful food, Freewheelin' Farm is also at the forefront of the growing movement toward community renewal, addressing issues of environment, health, and social equity through its on-farm education and policy work. The farm partners with youth organizations such as Food What in Santa Cruz to get its produce into schools, and it enthusiastically supports the regional FarmLink program, which received Federal Farm Bill funds to help with business planning and the purchase of a tractor. This all fits into a vision of sustainability that is for more than just the environment. All three farmers pursue off-farm income to get by, and the trio encourage each other to take sabbaticals every three years in order to make this venture a long-term sustained effort.

# Interview with Kirstin Yogg, Amy Courtney, and Darryl Wong

**How would you describe this area?**

**Kirstin Yogg, staff farmer**: We have two very different ecosystems happening within a few hundred feet. Our newest plot is not right on the cliff's edge overlooking the ocean but pretty darn close. The environment is fairly harsh—its very windy and it doesn't ever get that hot—so it's not an easy place to grow things. Then there's our little home farm, which is the sweetest little funky artistic warm spot.

**Amy Courtney, staff farmer**: All of this land was cultivated by old-time Italian farmers growing artichokes and then conventionally grown Brussels sprouts. The Bracero Barracks on the land next to us are remnants of that history, but slowly organics are spreading north up the coast. We're on this land because I used to work for a Swantonberry dairy farm that owned it. The owner had abandoned this acreage and I asked if I could work it.

**Darryl Wong, staff farmer**: The surrounding land is technically owned by the **Natural Resources Conservation Service** (NRCS) and the Coastal Commission. We are on this incredible coastline in California that draws so much tourism and offers so many benefits for people, yet we have an incredibly toxic agricultural practice that poisons it on a daily basis.

**How does the local economy impact your work?**

**AC**: Land prices and rents are insane! In the lifespan of this farm, it seems like people's discretionary income has gone down, down, down. In the '90s there was a lot of money and people lived large. At the same time, housing prices and rents continue to go up.

**Have you received loans or funding?**

**AC**: We need to buy another tractor, and there's some talk about applying for a loan to do that for this season, but we're only going to do that if we have to. We're thinking to buy it on a credit card and then let the **CSA** money pay for it. We'd all make a little less for the year, but it would get it done with.

**Do you have other jobs?**

**DW**: In the winter I work as a backyard tree pruner. It's somewhat of a specialized skill, and it's way more lucrative than farming.

**The Bracero Program**
The Bracero Program was a guest-worker program initiated in 1942 by the United States and Mexico. The demand for soldiers during WWII put pressure on agriculture such that the United States brought over four million Mexican men to work on farms. Many times these workers lived in substandard housing and were faced with unfulfilled contracts. *Bracero* is the Spanish word for "arm," which might have informed the title "farmhand."

Above:
(From left) Kirstin Yogg, Amy
Courtney, and Darryl Wong.

**KY**: I tend to do odds and ends during the wintertime. I definitely need to make money in other ways. There have been so many times when I've felt that if we could only make a good living doing this, it would feel so much easier. I love this work, but the financial piece of it is a struggle.

**Have you ever benefited from public policy?**

**AC**: One thing that is near and dear to me, that just got a little attention in the latest Farm Bill, is the work that California FarmLink is doing. They received a nod in the bill, and some money was put into their Individual Development Accounts (IDA) program. I applied and was forced to do cash-flow projections and make a business plan. It was a savings program whereby you would put in for two years and then they would return your money threefold at the end of the two years. After putting $100 per month into the savings plan, I came out with $10,000. This meant a tractor, which was a whole brand-new innovation out here. So, without that it might have been the end of Freewheelin' Farm.

**How does the biking aspect of the farm work, and how did it come about?**

**AC**: Agriculture is the second greatest petroleum-consuming industry in the United States. The vast majority of that consumption is in the delivery of food from farm to consumer. By minimizing our petroleum consumption in delivery down to a bottle of Tri-Flow every couple of years, we offer our modest attempt at addressing this resource consumption. Yes, it has it's challenges—more flat tires than your average truck delivery might encounter!—but it's often very enjoyable cruising down the Scenic Coast Highway at the end of a harvest day. When I arrive at the **CSA** pick-up, my heart is beating, my breath is full, and I feel great. Some people make a point

**FarmLink**

California FarmLink is a nonprofit organization that is part of a network of national FarmLink programs. Their primary focus is the transition of land from retiring farmers to younger farmers. Along with this handover, they facilitate mentorship, legal services, banking advice, loans, and business planning services.

The cropland in California is rapidly being developed into nonagricultural space, and farmers above the age of sixty-five far outnumber farmers under twenty-five. California FarmLink is engaged in fostering local, state, and national programs and policies to protect the remaining agricultural landscape and those who will tend to it.

to get some aerobic exercise in their daily schedule. We just make a point of incorporating that exercise into our weekly work schedule. It makes you show up for it every week!

A ripple effect is that many of our members are motivated to bike or walk from their homes to the pick-up sites in their neighborhoods. Therefore there's less petroleum consumption than had they driven to the store or other outlet, but, more important, it inspired them to pull out the old bike, or put the kids in the wagon and go for a walk, enjoy the journey, enjoy not being in their car on just another errand.

**DW**: We are such a blend of the ideal and the realistic. But I do feel like the biking, as unrealistic as it seems and idealistic as it is, is an important part for us. On the flipside, we need to be realistic, because if we are going to do this work we need to be able to make a living doing it and not kill ourselves year after year. That means buying tractors and getting bigger equipment, so that we're not using hand tools that we made ourselves.

**Where do you see Freewheelin' Farm in five years?**
**AC**: I'd like to see Freewheelin' fully using all our acreage; more and full-time youth projects; three routes twice a week with the bicycle; being financially sustainable; affording three health-care plans; having some actual legit paid people. I don't want to get bigger than where we are with the acreage—I think we are the right size for the people we are.

# Diggers' Mirth Collective Farm

Location:
**Burlington, Vermont**

Organizing body:
**5 partners, plus 2 employees**

Scale:
**10 acres**

Type:
**Co-op**

Currently producing:
**Mixed greens, plus 25 types of fruits and vegetables**

In operation:
**Since 1992**

Web site:
**intervale.org/list_of_farms/ index.shtml#diggers_mirth**

Diggers' Mirth Collective Farm takes its name from a radical agrarian movement that flourished briefly in England in the late 1640s and early 1650s, when a laborer named Gerrard Winstanley published a series of tracts challenging private property rights and arguing that "the earth . . . [was created] as a common storehouse for all."

Founded in 1992, the collective has comprised a total of eleven young farmers throughout the years. The farm is situated on ten acres within one of the nation's most successful farm incubator programs, Intervale Center. Intervale gives would-be farmers access to land, equipment, and training, and residents of Burlington, Vermont, gain access to great food and creative recycling programs. Diggers' Mirth sells 95 percent of all its produce within three miles of the farm. The farmers use their nearly broken truck to deliver to wholesale accounts three times a week, which include grocery stores and restaurants, in addition to two Saturday farmers' markets.

On the shores of Lake Champlain, at the foothills of the Green Mountains, Burlington is a small and grow-ing city with off-the-charts ratings on all quality-of-life measures. Collective member Elango Dev explains, "There are a lot of different opportunities here: markets, ethos, political temperament of the community. There are a lot of things cycling here in terms of food and food politics. People have been talking about these things for decades in Vermont. It has the price struc-ture of a college town, but not like Berkeley, California, where normal people are priced out."

A significant Somalian community has relocated to Burlington, and Diggers' Mirth employs two former farmers from Somalia.

Opposite, top:
Isha picking string beans.

Opposite, bottom:
A view of the Diggers' Mirth Collective Farm entrance.

# Interview with Dylan Zeitlyn

**How did the farm start?**

**Dylan Zeitlyn, collective member**: While I was in school at the University of California–Santa Cruz in 1992 studying argoecology, I went out to Vermont to do an apprenticeship at a community farm **CSA** at Intervale. While I was there I found out about its incubator farm that offered land to new farmers at a very low price, so I used my financial aid and grant money [that I never had to pay back] from school to start the farm.

**Can you talk about the collective aspect of the farm?**

It's fairly informal. There is an inertia to how things get done. We talk a lot in the field and make decisions while we are working. If you don't have a lot of meetings then things can evolve organically.

I have daily fantasies about having one acre and having it just be me. But I think it's good to have other people to be accountable to—it kind of keeps you in line. I'm better off being in a group because I can have crazy ideas, and they get hashed out by the group. I don't get self-destructive. I can't drag everyone down with me, because they won't let me.

**Do you connect with local initiatives or have you been involved with anything on a policy level?**

We were involved in starting the North End Farmers' Market in Burlington in 1992. We wanted to break the trend of having only one upscale market in town. The North End is a lower-income neighborhood with less access to fresh vegetables. Many Vietnamese and Middle Easterners live in that neighborhood. There are only about five other farms and some individual people selling at the market, but it is successful. We worked with the state to get Farm to Family farmers' market program coupons to be accepted at this market.

We also sell some of our produce to the Soup Mama project—a one-person pedal-powered soup delivery project in the North End.

**What are some of your challenges?**

We have flea beetles, the little jumpy black ones that put tiny holes in the kale. We use a mesh covering to keep them off—they're a real pain.

Opposite, clockwise from top left:
Dylan Zeitlyn with the weekly bean harvest.

Elango Dev with the weekly bean harvest.

Gray-water washing station.

The Diggers' Mirth washing station and toolshed.

**The Intervale Center**

This nonprofit, sustainable agri-cultural-based organization in Burlington, Vermont, emerged from discussions between a group of citizens and city officials who recognized the potential of an eco-park as a model of sustainable develop-ment. The Intervale Center manages 350 acres of farm-land, trails, wildlife corridors, a native plant nursery, and several programs along the Winooski River. The most successful program is its composting operation, which is the nation's largest example of an integrated regional organic recycling program. It handles twenty thousand tons of material annually and serves as a major source of revenue for the nonprofit. The group also hosts the Farms Program, a farm incubation program supporting beginning farmers by offering low-cost land, shared farm implements, storage, refrigeration, and business training.

Left:
Solar electric fence, to keep the deer out.

### Blight, late

Late Blight is a strain of the fungus Phytophthora infestans, which was responsible for the Irish potato famine in the nineteenth century. It is a disease that mainly attacks potatoes and tomatoes. During the summer of 2009, an outbreak hit the Northeast and the mid-Atlantic, believed to have spread from plants in garden stores to backyards and then to commercial fields. Once a crop is affected, it must be plowed under. Organic farmers are hit the hardest, as they do not use the herbicides that can be used to detour the fungus.

### The Chittenden Emergency Food Shelf (CEFS)

The Chittenden Emergency Food Shelf in Burlington, Vermont, is the largest direct-service emergency food provider in Vermont, and serves 11,300 people each year. The Chittenden Emergency Food Shelf relies on a broad base of community support to fund its programs. CEFS receives 60 percent of their support base from individuals, faith groups, local businesses, and other community organizations. The remainder comes through grants from the United Way and local towns and cities, as well as foundations.

Above:
Zeitlyn peers over a crop of tomatoes hit by summer 2009's late blight.

Another big problem here this year is that we got late blight on our tomato crop. We had to pull them all up and seal them in plastic so that the mold wouldn't spread, because it's airborne.

### Have you ever thought about making Diggers' Mirth products?

Yeah, we call those things labor-added products, but we try to stay low-maintenance. Through Intervale and the Food Shelf, there is a crew of gleaners that will come twice a week and pick anything extra.

### What's next for Diggers' Mirth Collective Farm?

We want to get more food out to the people, so we have this idea to put a rack on the side of the van with music and cruise around the neighborhood like an ice-cream truck.

# THE LONG HAUL

# The Acequiahood of the San Luis People's Ditch

Location:
**San Luis, Colorado**

Organizing body:
**16 *parcientes* (affiliated water users)**

Scale:
**Irrigation of approximately 2,100 acres of crops**

Type:
**Nonprofit**

Currently producing:
**Hay, alfalfa, chicos (dried corn), and squash**

In operation:
**Since 1852**

Web site:
**acequiainstitute.org**

Joe Gallegos, a sixth-generation acequia farmer, irrigates his land from the Rio Culebra watershed of the San Luis Valley of the Sangre de Cristo Mountain Range, which feeds the San Luis People's Ditch, the oldest "water right" in Colorado. His great-great-grandfather, Dario Gallegos, cofounded the People's Ditch in 1852, making his family owners of one of the longest continuously running farms in Colorado. Throughout his life, Joe Gallegos has been an activist in the historic acequia communities of the Rio Arriba—a seven-county area in south-central Colorado and northern New Mexico that is the headwaters of the Rio Grande system. The land they work and how they work it is unique in many ways. As Gallegos often remarks, it's been working for thousands of years, so why should it be changed?

What's working is both a technique and a way of looking at the world. Acequia farms rely on the gradual release of spring run-off water from winter snow pack, which feeds water naturally into local creeks and rivers. Using homemade diversion dams called "compuertas," the water is then channeled into ditches called "acequias." The acequias dissect the high point of a portion of unusually long plots of land, called "vara strips," which are the farms. Through an elaborate system of coordinating among neighbors, people who are close to one another because of their narrow lots cooperate to share resources. The ditches are filled on a schedule run by a *mayordomo* (ditch boss or ditch rider) who determines the schedule the farmers follow to flood the fields and irrigate crops. Beyond a complex physics experiment in gravity-fed irrigation that takes melting snow from a mountain and directs it into a field miles away, the process is a complex social organism—which takes a whole community to produce. Social scientists call this a modern "water democracy."

Devon G. Peña, a scholar raised in Laredo, Texas, has made it his mission to embed himself in the culture and politics of the acequia farmers in San Luis. He initially visited while teaching at a nearby college, bringing buses of students to the San Luis Valley for mobile classroom experiences to train future scholar-activists like himself. Peña met Gallegos during one of those trips and learned the ropes of the acequia culture from Joe and Joe's father. Throughout the years they worked together on farmers' cooperatives, built an acequia association for the region, and recently passed a law within state legislature that officially recognizes acequias and their approach to common ownership of water.

# Interview with Devon G. Peña and Joe Gallegos

**Please describe this bioregion.**

**Devon G. Peña, founder of the Acequia Institute and a scholar-activist-farmer**: It's the last place you would think agriculture would happen, because it's so high up: eight thousand feet above sea level. That's as high as Mt. Olympus.

But what people observe about this region is that you can walk through every major life zone in North America within a distance of a couple of miles, because you can go from eighteen thousand feet in elevation to four thousand within [that mileage]. It has an incredible range of altitude that gives it all these different life zones. And that's what makes this farming possible, too, because if not for the high mountain peaks and the deep snow pack, and the forests that protect that snow pack, allowing it to be slowly released over time, you couldn't irrigate here. You could practice dry agriculture, but you wouldn't be able to produce the food we do, because we are a spring-melt-dependent irrigation system and entirely driven by the accumulation and releases of the snow pack.

We have a sixty- to ninety-day growing season, so we have had to adapt our corn, our bean, our squash; they are all short-season lives. Which immediately gets us to politics and political cunning, because there are a lot of biotechnology companies that would love to get ahold of sixty-eight- to seventy-day corn. There aren't too many places that can say they have ninety-day corn. You have to do it quickly at eight thousand feet surrounded by fourteen-thousand-foot mountains!

Each bioregion is culturally distinct, with its own cultural heritage as well. This area is considered by many to be the mystical homeland of the Aztecs: Aztlán.

**Tell me about water, your relationship to it, and the logic behind the Acequiahood.**

**Joe Gallegos, acequia farmer**: My dad once told me, "Let the water tell you what to do." And I wonder about the political aspect of that: Does the water tell you to dam it? We have a tendency not to let the water tell us what to do; instead we try to control it.

**DP**: We try to move it uphill toward money, defy the laws of gravity instead of listening to the water!

**Aztlán**

During the rise of the Chicano movement in the 1960s, Aztlán became a symbol of the Chicano struggle to reunify with the land, to restore land rights, to restore all the lost land grants that became part of the public domain of the United States. It has significant meaning to people of Meso-american descent—those from the Aztec, Maya, and Inca regions stretching from Mexico through much of Central America and parts of South America—but specifically refers to the land of the Aztecs. In the southwestern United States, many of the national forests, the Bureau of Land Management areas, and National Park Service lands were originally Mexican and Spanish landmasses that became enclosed, privatized, or put into public domain.

Above:
Pena irrigates Joe Gallegos'
corn field; the orange "tarpolio"
controls water flow from one
farm to the next.

Part of the success of the acequia system is that it's based on human modesty;
we are humble before the power of nature, and therefore our control of water is
incomplete. I've described it as sort of how a beaver works. We don't control our
water very well. It leaks all over the place. But it's that leaking that's created this
oasis! That wouldn't have happened if we had cement-lined and piped everything.

If the water wants to go and create a wetland over there, you let it create that
wetland. In doing that, you're creating habitat for wildlife. You're supporting migra-
tory species, because they have a place to sit down and rest and get some food.
So I like to describe us as equal-opportunity providers, because it is precisely the
acequia's economic inefficiency that makes possible this bounty of biodiversity—
we don't deny water to wild plants or animals. And that leads to a lot of geo-
political conflict, because we are in a way undermining the fundamental rules of
Western water law by behaving the way we do.

Ever since the 1880s, we've been fighting off the modern state and court system
that has viewed us as primitive, backward, inefficient. There's a book called *History
of Agriculture in Colorado*, published in 1926 by what became Colorado State
University Ag School [now the CSU College of Agricultural Sciences] and written
by Alvin T. Steinel. It reads: "Under Spanish Americans, agriculture did not progress."
So we've been fighting not only a new law [and] a legal system that we see as

incompatible with our original system of water law, we're also fighting these stereotypes in the media, in policy-making circles, in the courts. The things judges have said about us over the years are amazing! "It's time to bring these Mexicans into the twentieth century," one judge said, because we were asking for the restoration of our common-use rights. So the battle here has always been not just about the conditions that make farming possible, but the ways in which we are perceived as a threatening, unassimilable "other."

**How have you taken these ways of working—things you've learned from the acequia—and applied them into other parts of life? Is the acequia a model that can be transferred?**
**JG**: I was once approached by a commissioner who was interested in using the Acequiahood as a model for negotiations. Acequia farmers have to negotiate all the time—it's how we really try to avoid having to go to water court, which we hate. We've been called "radical" before, but we're not radical—this has always been the way it's been done.

**DP**: My understanding of the true meaning of "radical" is "back to the roots" . . . we never left our roots, so we're not radical, we're all ready there.

The first thing to recognize is that you don't have to manage a ditch on the basis of individual utility. You can do it on the basis of mutual reliance and interest. There are alternative rationalities that create economic relationships that don't depend on individual and utilitarian interest. It's the collective interest of acequia that guides us all, and it requires an immense level of social interaction and cooperation to work. So you have to be very patient, and you have to really know each other as well. You can't be strangers, because it requires constant sacrifice and waiting for your turn. Because of that mutual-reliance interest, you create a certain code of behavior that a lot of communities would find hard to reproduce.

Now, the rules of the acequia could be exported. A rule that works really well for us is that the ditch is considered a community resource rather than a private property, and the water is considered a community resource rather than a commodity. For example, at the beginning of every spring, we have to clean up the ditch together, which is a cooperative labor that is required by our law.

**What motivated you to look to public policy to support your work here?**
**DP**: Well, because it was all informal, it wasn't the law. We had a law that was different from our informal practices. So our law survived through informal practice.

Opposite, clockwise from top: *La Vega*, meaning "The Meadow" in Spanish, is also known as The Commons because it is customarily used just like the water—anyone in the acequiahood may graze their cows on La Vega.

This oven is used for roasting chicos, the arid-weather corn of the region. Roasting is a communal activity each season when farmers and friends help each other pack the ovens with corn husks. The roasted chicos are then sold whole-sale and kept as staple foods for the winter months.

Adelmo Kaber is an elder and a teacher to local farmers.

Seed saving is done informally by Acequiahood farmers. They hope that their cooperative will help to coordinate sharing and preserving the seeds.

The work of Devon G. Peña, a farmer and renowned scholar studying environmental justice, straddles academy and the acequia.

But as long as it's informal, there's always the threat that the state is going to force you to do it the other way. And so I think there were a lot of events that convinced us that we needed to get a new water law passed.

For instance, there was a ruling in a divorce case—handled by the water judge who was also the divorce judge—that granted the water to the wife and the land to the husband, and that's against our customary law. We cannot separate the water from the land. It's a place-based asset, it's here to be used for acequia purposes only. Of course, it turned out the wife wanted to sell the land to a nonagricultural user for a subdivision. So we had to mobilize; we bought those water rights to keep them in the acequia.

In the meantime, we worried that more defections could occur, more divisions of water from the land, and we needed to prevent that from happening. So in 1998, Joe and I created the Acequia Association. It took eleven years of organizing the acequia community, and then getting one of us elected to the state legislature, before any policy was passed—the Acequia Recognition Law (HB 09-1233), signed by the governor in April of 2009.

**What are you trying to accomplish with the Acequia Institute?**
**DP**: The idea for the Acequia Institute is twofold. One is to promote research on sustainable agriculture and food justice in acequia communities by funding graduate student research. Every year, we fund three grad students doing research, and it has to be participatory, collaborative-action research led by the farmers, directed by the farmers.

Then the other thing we do is fund three **food-justice co-ops**, all women-led: Community to Community (C2C) in Bellingham, Washington, the South Central Farmers in Los Angeles/Bakersfield, and then a local program called the Novela Project, which makes a link between elder acequia farmers and youth. We're teaching youth about acequia irrigation methods and practices and addressing the food-sovereignty and heritage-cuisine needs of the elders, who have very poor access to fresh fruits and vegetables. So the Institute exists to bring together research, advocacy, and social action at the local grassroots level. That's where we're at, at this point.

**Where do you want to see the Acequiahood in five years? Where do you want to see the community?**
**DP**: I don't want to see the Family Dollar open here!

Top, left:
The Acequia ditch and
Joe Gallegos.

Top, right:
The Acequiahood at work.
Cooperation among neighboring farmers is crucial to the
functioning of the farm.

Bottom:
Sandra J. Santa Cruz regards
modern chute and channel
upgrades to the ancient
acequia ditch.

**JG**: Yeah, I don't either.

**DP**: This is still a community that's off the map. You have to travel forty-five miles to get fast food. I very much want to see this remain a slow, local, and deep-food community five years from now. It's not enough to be slow and local, we also have to recognize the need for a deep sense of place, for deep respect of local, space-based ecological wisdom. When you arrive at that, then you can really begin to negotiate sustainable agriculture without losing sight of the social-justice dimension.

Climate change will surely affect political dynamics in the coming years, certainly in the next fifty. We're going to see major hydrological shifts occurring in this entire bioregion, and that's why one of the things we're doing through the Acequia Institute is trying to develop drought resistance through the use of roasting white corn. I got a white flint from people in Baja, California, that you don't even have to irrigate for it to produce corn, and so I'm trying to hybridize it with local chicos because they share a lot of texture qualities, and they're both short seeds and varieties, and they're not water hogs. Our local corn probably consumes one-tenth as much water as Midwestern corn, due to our irrigations.

The ruthless commodification of everything must be met with the decommodifica-tion of the most basic thing, which is food, which becomes part of a web of social relationships instead of just a market product, or a thing with a price.

It's really more of a way of life than an occupation, to be an Acequia farmer. You're not going to make money. It's not about money—it's about a way of life that's very connected to place, and, therefore, with that connection comes a lot of responsi-bility. You've got to keep the place beautiful and healthy for your next generation. That was always a strong ethic of this community. But it's not a utopia—we may be a model, but we're riddled with contradictions of class, of gender, of race. But I do think it's a model that has worked well for thousands of years. And I think [that's because there's] basically one difference in the rules: individual versus mutual-reliance interests. If we can learn to have a conversation about which of those models we want to be the basis of our economic paradigm, we're going to be forced to conclude it ain't capitalism! I don't know what we would call it, but . . .

**Acequiahood?** [laughter]

**DP**: Acequianomics.

# South Central Farmers

Location:
**Bakersfield and Los Angeles, California**

Organizing body:
**5 staff and 15 families**

Scale:
**80 sharecropped acres and 85 owned acres**

Type:
**Worker owned and operated**

Currently producing:
**Kale, melons, squash, beets, carrots, Armenian cucumbers, and tomatoes**

In operation:
**Since 2003**

Web site:
**southcentralfarmers.com**

Following the 1992 riots in south-central Los Angeles, a group of mostly indigenous people from Mexico living in the area came together to start the largest urban farm in the country. In 2006, those farmers were evicted from the fourteen acres of South Central Farm (SCF) following a highly complex series of events wherein real-estate developers, other rivaling community organizations, and corrupt local politicians plotted to reverse the original agreements for using the land. Calls for solidarity and support poured in from all over the world. The event became a focal point for urban agriculture, land use, and self-sufficiency activists.

Eventually the eviction process was completed, and the loose-knit group was without land. Recently some of the farmers have leased land one hundred miles north in Bakersfield, California. Although they no longer farm in Los Angeles, they maintain roots in that community. Their work has taken on a new dimension trying to survive as a **CSA** and market farm.

The incredible intersection of people who reached out to SCF during its eviction reveal how many people can unite around a common idea. And it also reveals that no matter how much solidarity you have, things don't always work out in favor of the majority of the people, or on the side of the ones with the most support. But the farmers from South Central Farm have persevered, and reinvented themselves.

Tezozomoc (Tezo) is a second-generation South Central Farmer. His father was an original organizer when SCF first began fourteen years ago. By day he works as an engineer, and any free time is spent organizing and coordinating with others to get out to their land in Bakersfield, a long trek from their homes in Los Angeles. Tezo has incredible enthusiasm and energy, and moves from speaking very concretely in terms of the land, the eviction, the food, and the community to making theoretical references that draw from an incredible array of influences—a testament to his versatility as a thinker and organizer.

# Interview with Tezozomoc

**If South Central Farm was offered property in Los Angeles, would the group take it?**
**Tezozomoc, elected representative**: I would take it, but I would keep the land in Bakersfield—the armpit of California—as well. The need is so bad for good food in the city. We need this scale of working. I think that this whole idea that agribusiness is going to solve our problems is just not going to happen.

**What's the challenge of having healthful food in your part of Los Angeles?**
In South Central L.A., there are food deserts with twenty-eight thousand liquor stores, one grocery store, and no markets in one zip code. My criticism of the 5 A Day program is that you can't say "Eat fruits!" when they aren't there.

**Has the land in Bakersfield affected what you are growing?**
We had to adapt to the land and to the weather, since it's more than one hundred degrees [Fahrenheit] a lot of the time. We don't try to change the land to work with our desires, we grow for the conditions that the land and weather provide.

We bring seeds from Mexico and collect them and distribute them. Kale is not a standard staple in the Mexican diet, but we are turning the people on to it. Once you show them how to use it, and once they know it is just cabbage in leaf form, they will eat it. It is one of our most productive products.

**What are your growing methods?**
We are certified organic, but we don't do anything that we haven't been doing for thousands of years. I tell people we have been growing organic for fifteen thousand years before there was a **USDA**. These agencies of legitimacy are a bureaucratic farce, but we have to do it. I mean, I don't want to call a watermelon an apparatus or a water capturer so that it makes you feel good and coerces you to exchange more capital. I don't want to engage in a branding strategy. I could say these are "Mesoamerican" whatever, but then I am doing what everyone else is doing. This is the antithesis of what Foucault says about the René Magritte painting: "'This is not a pipe,' this is not a pipe: the painting, written sentence, drawing of a pipe—all this is not a pipe."

One of the most important lessons we learned from Mark Halsey [author of *Deleuze and Environmental Damage: Violence of the Text*] is questioning the definition of sustainable. To me, "sustainability" is the collective knowledge that

**5 A Day**
Following recommendations by the World Health Organization for individuals to consume at least four hundred grams of vegetables daily, the international 5 A Day program—especially widespread in the United States and the United Kingdom—is designed to encourage the consumption of at least five portions of fruit and vegetables each day.

Above:
(From left) Liberio Tlatoa, Jose
Luis Moran, and Ubaldo Tlatoa.

we have of twenty thousand years of farming that has been handed down for generations. I don't do anything different than my grandfather does. I have not adapted any of these so-called "**permaculture**" strategies. I am not knocking them, but, for me, sustainability is a deeper question: Are we sustaining the exchange? Or are we sustaining the producer? Or the people involved in the process?

**What are some of the roles of people involved in the process?**
There are ten to fifteen families. We work two parts: distribution and farming. We do about fifty acres with four full-time people and on weekends volunteers from student groups come help with the harvesting.

**Do you have your own fleet of trucks?**
Yeah, we have two sixteen-foot trucks and two refrigerated vans. We support eight farmers' markets in L.A. and operate a **CSA** program. And recently Whole Foods has started picking up our products.

**How far is your distribution right now?**
One hundred twenty miles. We have to stay within the food shed, which is two hundred miles. But ideally I would love to be in the middle of downtown L.A. But with politics being what they are, we've scared a lot of people. A lot of people won't even touch us. I am surprised Whole Foods is willing to, but we have such a good product, and customers love it. We've been very consistent, and we separate the cooperative part of our politics.

**What are the biggest costs?**
Diesel from driving, electricity, water, and 20 percent of what we make goes to the landlord we rent from. At the moment, we are still locked into private land. But we own an eighty-five-acre farm ten miles away, though we don't have a pump for the well there, so we have to work here until we have the $100,000 we need to pay for the pump. Eventually, we want to put a farmhouse on that land so we can have a place to live when we work.

**Would you ever take out a loan?**
The whole idea is to constitute our own economic system. That has to happen without loans because loans are basically forms of capture—you're not working for you, you're working for someone else.

Opposite, clockwise from top: The South Central School Bus heads out after a long day.

Tony Lopez gives his impressions of the heat, the stars at night, and how the hard work of farming is humbling. He is one of several Movimiento Estudiantic Chicano de Aztlán (MEChA) students from Pasadena who volunteered during the summer of 2009.

MEChA volunteers assemble boxes.

An Armenian cucumber harvested by one of the MEChA students.

Left:
Hand-harvesting and bunching carrots is like finding little colorful gems that emerge from within a waist-high patch of weeds.

Below:
Miquel Tomas hydrates and cools off by the melons.

Opposite:
Liberio Tlatoa heads out for the long haul back to Los Angeles. He may get to bed at 2 A.M., then he'll get up at 4 A.M. to hit the road back up to Bakersfield.

Above:
Ubaldo Tlatoa, Rose "Xochit" Lujan, and Tezo prepare for the Hollywood Farmers' Market.

Right:
Harvesting and bunching beets by hand.

**The Immigration Reform and Control Act**
IRCA is an act of Congress defined in 1986 that reformed United States immigration law, making it illegal to knowingly hire or recruit illegal immigrants (immigrants who do not possess lawful work authorization). In addition, the act required employers to attest to their employees'immigration status and granted amnesty to certain illegal immigrants who entered the United States before January 1, 1982, and had resided here continuously. The act also granted a path toward legalization to certain agricultural seasonal workers and immigrants who had been continuously and illegally present in the United States since January 1, 1982.

**Do you work around any policy initiatives?**
Policy to normalize me doesn't help me, or policy that puts me in jail doesn't help me, but policy that gives me critical freedom . . . that I am interested in. Policy is nothing more than a normalizing agent that is imposed on people. I want to deconstruct policy so that it can be an element that gives you critical freedom.

One thing we have been dealing with is the Immigration Reform and Control Act (IRCA) that says you don't have the right to work unless it is granted to you by the state. We have been tackling immigration rights and what "immigration rights" means. For me, I have conflicting emotions about these things. That needs to be deconstructed.

**What impresses you the most about working on South Central Farm?**
Farming is a high-skilled practice. Farming is like philosophy; it's a creative practice. Philosophers create concepts and farmers create food, and it's not a single discipline—you have to be a chemist, physicist, mathematician, meteorologist.

# On-the-Fly Farm

Location:
**Union Pier, Michigan**

Organizing body:
**1 farmer, with occasional
help from friends**

Scale:
**5 acres**

Type:
**For profit**

Currently producing:
**Bok choy, eggplant, kale,
and potatoes**

In operation:
**Since 2004**

Web site:
**chicorycenter.org**

Longtime activist David Meyers has bounced among artist communities, low-income neighborhoods, and community organizations, fighting for their rights to be a neighborhood, a sovereign nation, and community gardens. His eclectic interests, intense personality, and high energy level keep him on the move—and his moves are on-the-fly, thus the name of his farming endeavor based in southwestern Michigan since 2004: On-the-Fly Farm.

A South Bend, Indiana, native, Meyers moved to nearby Chicago to study creative writing and journalism—a practice he maintains through an active blog about his unique Midwestern activism, his fair-trade coffee-roasting business, and life between the big city where his community remains and life on the rural farm growing potatoes and salad mixes for **CSA** subscribers.

As an anarchist, Meyers has also committed himself to not paying taxes to the government that go to fund wars. The principle most central to his work is that of solidarity—the goal of self-reliant communities and communities of support and care across class divisions.

# Interview with David Meyers

**When did On-the-Fly Farm start?**
**David Meyers, founder**: It came from an act of brutal police violence that was directed at me on July 23, 1994. I tend to act with a degree of anger as my motivation. And On-the-Fly Farm comes partly out of that.

I started working on community gardens in Chicago a month or two after having suffered this police brutality. It was a major way of grounding myself. It came out of a spirit of anarchist direct action and experience doing organizing and solidarity work. The Greenhouse Garden was in a city-owned lot—we never asked anyone for permission. My friend Amir Hampton and I set up a recycling program, and the kids would run around the alleys and collect stuff. We set up a compost bin. It was an amazing after-school program with no kind of funding from anyone. It also performed a kind of babysitting service for a lot of moms in the area. This was all incidental. We didn't have this in mind. But it was a great experience for us and the dozens of kids who were involved. That garden turned into a battle of owner-ship. The city government knew that if we didn't get to keep our garden there we would dig up the sidewalks with jackhammers. We got a thousand signatures on a petition, plus signatures from businesspeople. And eventually the city gave it to us.

The history of the Greenhouse Garden is the history of the gentrification of Wicker Park. That's not necessarily a good history. But the garden is still there. It's not completely gentrified or yuppified, but the area certainly is.

In 1999, I collaborated with Alejandrina Torres, a Puerto Rican political prisoner pardoned by President Clinton, who really needed to ground herself after being incarcerated. Together we reignited the El Coquí garden in Humboldt Park [in Chicago]. I have a strong belief in grounding as a way to overcome adversity. It was something I really understood when working with youth. I talked to so many youth who benefited from some kind of grounding on land. It's intimately tied to issues of gentrification. If you feel tied to some degree to the actual land beneath your feet, like Humboldt Park for example, then you are much more likely to fight to keep it.

**By this point, were you working in that neighborhood?**
I started working in Humboldt Park as a grant writer at the Puerto Rican Cultural Center (PRCC) in 1995. But aside from working with some youth from the PRCC high school, I ultimately found the grant writing part to be one of the most boring

Right:
David Meyers (in white) of On-the-Fly Farm is joined by (from left) Eric Brose, Jennifer Starkovsky, and Sarah Jean McHugh of Foxglove CSA, who also work a plot of Hidden Haven land.

things on Earth—it is something you could probably train bonobos, monkeys, or chimps to do. So I had this idea to start some kind of rural outpost or retreat center. The basic idea was to "feed the people, feed the revolution." [The outpost] would feed a social-change movement leading toward revolution that didn't have a lot of not-for-profit constraints set up around it.

**What happened between this time period and today that led you to get your own farm?**

I saw a lot of problems with the rapidity of gentrification in Chicago. The idea of working on land that was going to be under threat of development was a really tiresome idea to me. So I decided to step out of Chicago for a while. The ideas started to simmer during the next couple of years. i had some extra income to get access to land, so I rented twenty-three acres from a woman in southwestern Michigan who was going to be out of town for a year and needed someone to stay on her land in Berrien County, one of the largest fruit-producing counties in the country. The house was insanely gorgeous and the land was mystically beautiful. I drove out there to start farming on April 30, 2004.

The land had not been farmed conventionally for at least twenty years. It was really well taken care of. It was a little bit hilly, which is not common in this flat land. It was really clean and not toxic. The soil was really dense, as most is in the Midwest, and a bit sandy because it's close to Lake Michigan.

I purchased a rototiller on eBay and started to work. It was a very late start date for farming and for starting to grow food. But I was extremely motivated and had an insane amount of energy. I started rototilling and the chain snapped off. Since I didn't want to spend the day dealing with a small engine repair place, I just started digging with a shovel. I dug up probably the equivalent of a city lot that afternoon. That took a lot of energy, because it was really hard sod. I was nuts.

Two days later, I wondered how I would get the produce out to people. I had heard of the **CSA** model, and so I sat down and in four minutes had written a letter to friends: "On-the-Fly Farm CSA—Starts July 1st—You Wanna Join?" and I got all ten subscribers right away, each paying $150 for the season. And that structure has stayed basically the same since.

From the start, I wanted a part of this farm to be about solidarity. I was concerned about who gets to eat this fresh organic and healthful food. I think about this a lot. I decided that a certain percentage of what I am growing needs to be used to challenge unequal structures of food consumption and distribution. I still had strong ties with Humboldt Park. So the first **CSA** subscribers were informed that part of their participation was subsidizing my work to get 20 to 30 percent of the food to low-income people in Humboldt Park and some in Little Village.

I knew this project had to have a political dimension as well. And that meant locally in the region where the farm was, as well as an urban-rural connection between Chicago and this place. At the same time I had a coffee-roasting hobby. I would later raise several thousand dollars in legal funds to support a friend and local seeking political asylum by selling this coffee.

**How did you transition from the first farm to the current farm at Hidden Haven?**
The first farm generated a lot of activity. People who were in the **CSA** came out to work, and different groups used the house for retreats. But when the landowner returned at the end of that year, a lot of things fell apart simultaneously. It became clear that it was going to be hard to stay on the land. I had also just gone through a breakup. And to add to it all, I had lost 90 percent of my income because the IRS put levies on my consultant pay from the PRCC, which was subsidizing this project, resulting from my practice of tax resisting. Even though everything was crashing at the end of 2004, I somehow managed to do a second year of the **CSA** through subsidies from other small farmers in the area. That has always been a part of my interest, to connect with other people who are good at growing food but not interested in or able to be into marketing. I would pay them and put their food in the **CSA** box. In total, I was there fifteen months, enough to farm two seasons.

At the end of 2005, I happened to stumble across a listing buried on the Land Connection Web site that read "farmers looking for land and landowners looking for farmers"—there really needs to be a Craigslist for this kind of farm situation; you could facilitate so much land reform informally!

**On-the-Fly Budget 2009**

| Expenses | Income |
|---|---|
| $2,400 Transportation (car, gas, insurance) | CSA Subscriptions (22 x $400) $8,800 |
| $500 Seeds, potatoes, onions | Market sales $1,000 |
| $400 Fertilizer, lime | Donations $500 |
| $200 Supplies, tools | Solidarity subsidy $700 |
| $900 Eggs, pickles, fruit, etc. | |
| $100 Fees, memberships | |
| $6,500 Farmer pay (1,040 hours [26 weeks x 40 hours] = $6.25/hr) | |
| **$11,000** | **$11,000** |

Above:
An On-the-Fly farmer looks out over the fields.

**Is there something that you've grown that you have a special relationship with?**
From the get-go, the thing I love to grow the most is the potato. The potato is not the easiest thing to grow, especially by hand, because there is a lot of digging involved in the front end and the back. But for someone who wants to get grounded, it's the best. Men love it. Women who want to use their big muscles love it. Troubled youth love it. There is an endorphin change that happens when you exert yourself that much.

A third of what I plant is potatoes, two hundred fifty pounds of them. That means digging a trench by hand that is a half-mile long. That is a lot of digging, and that gives you a lot of time to think.

Above:
Landowners Joyce and Jim Mims walk the land with David Meyers of On-the-Fly Farm.

**Just Farming at Hidden Haven**

Starting in 2005, Chicago-area attorney Joyce Mims offered land that she owned, Hidden Haven Farm, an hour and a half from the city in Union Pier, Michigan, to two different agriculture initiatives based in Chicago. The two projects grew out of different contexts, both with a commitment to social justice. One was On-the-Fly Farm, a project of long-time anarchist organizer, fair-trade coffee roaster, and tax-resister David Meyers. The other was God's Gang, initiated by Carolyn Thomas along with family and friends, whose mission was to distribute and grow food for the displaced residents of the Chicago Housing Authority's Robert Taylor Homes. Eventually the two organizations would be joined by Foxglove Farm in 2008, an initiative of Sara Jean McHugh and Eric Brose from Chicago, and the Lampkins, a family from nearby northern Indiana that

raises horses. These diverse groups would come to share land, resources, and ideas.

In the mid-1990s, Mims purchased the acreage for her horses. The land's potential grew in her imagination as she envisioned leaving her corporate job to become a farmer. She attempted to farm full time for a few years but eventually went back to work. After a couple of years of weekend farming, she decided it was no longer viable for her financially. The back and forth between her job, coping with the restaurant that purchased her produce, and farm work was too much. But unwilling to let her land languish, Mims posted an announcement to TheLand Connection.org, hoping to attract a farmer who would treat the land responsibly. In fact, she was willing to offer the land for free. For years, nobody responded.

Finally, in 2005, David Meyers excitedly called Mims, responding to her posting.

Almost simultaneously a secretary at Mims's job started telling her about God's Gang and their need for land. Coincidentally, Meyers and Thomas had been in conversation about farming together the year before—then, independently of one another, they happened to contact Mims the same week. As Meyers recalls, "Joyce liked all of us, and so we all decided to go for it!"

The two groups began cultivating plots and developing skills side by side, fundraising under the name Just Farming Small Farmers Confederation. Hailing from different communities, subcultures, and worldviews, they literally found common ground at Hidden Haven.

# God's Gang

Location:
**Chicago and Dawson, Illinois, and Union Pier, Michigan**

Organizing body:
**Varies based on projects and available funds**

Scale:
**Multiple sites, including urban backyard gardens throughout Chicago, farmers' markets, greenhouses on the south and west sides of Chicago, a rural animal farm (Karaal Farm) in Dawson, Illinois, and crops in Union Pier, Michigan (at Hidden Haven)**

Type:
**Nonprofit**

Currently producing:
**Worms, cotton, geese, ducks, tilapia, and gourds**

In operation:
**Since the mid-1970s**

Web site:
**Godsgang1.net**

"No Child Left Inside" is Carolyn Thomas's motto, borrowed from former President Bush's education policy No Child Left Behind. There is not a better example of diligence toward this maxim than her organization, God's Gang.

The group grew out of an impulse to connect with kids in a neighborhood that was largely abandoned by the world around it. Kids have always been at the center of God's Gang's work, making space for their growth and their development as people. They started as a dance group and then morphed into a food pantry, a library, and then a fish and worm farm inside abandoned public-housing units. The group was displaced from its facilities numerous times in what has come to be known unofficially as "urban removal" and officially as the "Plan for Transformation" of nearly all of the city's public-housing units into market-rate homes. The age of state welfare is over, and subsidized, low-income residents are being flung into the city's private-housing market to compete with everyone else.

In the midst of this mass displacement, the community cultivated by God's Gang is also being flung in many directions. But their commitment and savviness earned them access to rural land in Union Pier, Michigan—land they share with On-the-Fly Farm. Their headquarters are now located in Thomas's backyard in the far south-side Chicago neighborhood of Roseland. Greater emphasis is being placed on working with individual families to have backyard gardens or visits to the farmland for an escape from the city.

# Interview with Carolyn Thomas

**Tell us how God's Gang came about.**

**Carolyn Thomas, founder**: We started God's Gang at St. Mary's church in the Washington Park area of Chicago in an effort to try to get kids to stop fighting so much. It was the mid-1970s. People who came to the church had been displaced by the building of Robert Taylor Homes, nearby public-housing projects. We started by getting kids interested in break-dancing after church. Then we started a breakfast program. People would give us commodities, but we wouldn't serve them—we wouldn't serve rice or grits. We'd serve pancakes with syrup, strawberries, and whipped cream. We just made elaborate, crazy stuff. And people would come!

Once we had a Halloween party. We had a huge pumpkin that was the prize for who could dance the best. I remember a kid saying, "We're just like the other gangs, only we're God's gang." And that was how we got our name.

Then we wondered how we could get the kids to stay longer at the church. We decided that we could do some gospel dancing—not "praise dancing." The kids would get a record, or Scripture, and they would make their own movements to it. Then other churches started to invite us to perform. We performed in parks and did Juneteenth celebrations.

Then we started doing black history in our own community-centered way. We would ask the kids to find the oldest person they knew in their family or in the neighborhood, and they were to ask that person for the oldest thing they had and bring it back so we could make an exhibit together. We would always get amazing things, sometimes stuff we didn't even know [the name of] or how it was used. At some point, we asked the kids, "If there was one thing that you didn't have to worry about all day long, one thing that you think all of us together have the power to solve, what would it be?" And they said "food." So we opened a food pantry and called it Mother's Cupboard.

Eventually we got a grant from the Chicago Area Projects for $2,000, as well as a promise of space in a Chicago Housing Authority (CHA) building. We waited months. Finally, the manager offered us a five-room apartment, which we divided into different food rooms, and we just went from there.

Above:
The core group of God's Gang families and volunteers pose in Carolyn Thomas's (center) backyard in Roseland, near the southern edge of Chicago.

**Where were you getting food from at that point?**

We got food from the Chicago Food Depository. We had no staff—we relied totally on volunteers. Seniors and people who didn't work, and those who were on assistance, would run the pantry until the kids got out of school and we got off work in the evenings. An AmeriCorps friend would loan us trucks and volunteers for deliveries. That's how we started, moving forty-three thousand pounds of food; the depository gave us the "Pantry of the Year" award that year.

Later Philip Morris USA approached us and offered us a grant after taking a tour of our operation. That's how we got our truck. We've never really written proposals, because people just helped us.

**How did people find out about God's Gang at this point?**

We got very good publicity after moving so many pounds of food that first year with mostly children. We ran out of food after our first grant of $2,000—food was seven cents a pound—we were giving it away so fast.

I think right about there we were a twinkle in Phoebe Griswold's eye; she was the director of the Chicago office of **Heifer Project International** and had dreamed of an urban ag program.

**Is this when you made the shift from food distribution to food production?**
Yes, it was around 1998 or '99. You have to have livestock to work with Heifer
Project International. They introduced us to raising worms and fish indoors, and
we got space from CHA with new floors, new lights, new everything.

I worked as a United States postal worker and so I lobbied the American Postal
Workers Union to donate to us their employee library, since it wouldn't be needed
in the new building they were moving to. They agreed. They had desks, every
reference volume you could think of, the complete works of [Edgar Allan] Poe. It
was marvelous. We got trucks and moved the library to our new space and started
offering homework help in addition to all the food-related work.

Then we asked for a third space, because we needed windows and natural light
for the fish. We had been bugging Ed Moses, the head of public relations for CHA
at the time, about this for a while. Then one day we had a residents' party and he
came to visit. I was reading *Amistad* to two children when he came through that
day. He said, "This is beautiful!" Then he turned to leave, and he looked to the
left. It was where we kept our thirty bins of worms, two fish systems, and three
fifty-five-gallon bubbling drums. He looked at Ms. Moore, one of the elders and
a resident, and he said, "Ms. Moore, did anyone ever tell you that water and books
don't mix?" And she said, "We've been asking for months for the other space,
but nobody would give it to us, so we had to put our fish in here, in our library."
The next day, the CHA built the worms- and fish-farms space.

In the new space, we increased to six fish systems—it was really great. I think
we also got maybe one hundred beds of worms. A carpenter was helping
us put in more windows—and the next day we were told that our building was
coming down.

That's when we started working with the Jewish Council on Urban Affairs to try to
save the building. We started spending all of our time trying to stop the demolition
of 5266 South State Street. It came down to the last fourteen families in the God's
Gang building, and we were holding out. The head of CHA came to us and said,
"I don't know where you are going, but you got to get the hell out of here." Every-
one told us that we had to go, but Ms. Moore was holding out. My sister would sit
with her while I was at work. Then some folks from the Coalition to Protect Public
Housing would stay all night, every night. We were there twenty-four hours a day.
We even filed a lawsuit to try to keep the building open, but that didn't work.
Finally CHA threatened that if we did not leave then we would lose the library, the

**Coalition to Protect Public Housing**
Founded in 1996 in response
to the federal mandate to
demolish public housing
nationwide, 18,000 of those
units in Chicago, CPPH is an
advocacy group of public-
housing residents, community-
based organizations, religious
institutions, businesses, and
nonprofit organizations. In
recent years, their work has
changed to focus on Human
Rights Violations as the
Chicago Housing Authority's
Plan for Transformation has
reached its conclusion. The
CPPH has cited the plan as
a failure and a human rights
violation because one-to-one
replacement housing has not
been provided for all residents
who were displaced because
of the demolitions.

Top:
Students from a City of Chicago After School Matters program work at 2626 East 83rd Street in Chicago.

Bottom, right:
Carolyn Thomas poses with a goose in her backyard. God's Gang started keeping livestock when Heifer International approached them about a funding opportunity for their food-related work in public housing in Chicago.

Bottom, left:
God's Gang teens in the After School Matters program bring the oldest greenhouse in Southside Chicago back to life.

pantry, and the worm and fish farms. When they moved the security—the police had been there all this time—people started breaking in. They stole the copper out of the huge new refrigerators and freezers. They broke through the walls and took everything of value. They destroyed our computers—the scavengers just took over. It was crazy. And then they set all the worms out.

**Someone from CHA did that?**

Yeah, someone from CHA moved our worms out into the street. The only thing that saved them was that, the week prior, kids had come for training and had over-bedded them. So we didn't lose them—they didn't die, they didn't freeze.

Then the *Chicago Tribune* wrote about [the incident], and the very next day we moved the worm beds into someone's apartment. We didn't have the library—it had been destroyed. The food pantry went to a church—it was just a mess.

We just prayed, and didn't worry about it, and one day, somebody gave Ms. Moore a key. Turns out the CHA officials built us a brand-new $35,000 worm and fish farm. We had the entire first floor. It had twelve windows.

But the overall Plan for Transformation was still taking place, and the building with our new facility was still slated to be demolished. A meeting was set up between our kids and the new head of CHA. He was totally impressed by our work and offered to give us one of the thousands of buildings they had around the city for a dollar. We tried to take them up on this but every time we found [a building that] we liked, there was some obstacle or reason why it wouldn't work. Eventually when they were ready to evict us again we sued. But the legal battle dragged on so long, and meanwhile our families were being displaced throughout the city, and every-one was really challenged by all of this. So I called our lawyer and asked him to settle the lawsuit. We settled out of court for one-fourth of what an independent group had appraised all the work and the work we could have done was worth—something like a million dollars. We were without a home and we spent most of the settlement money in the first three years just trying to hold on to all of our fish, worms, and gardening equipment in storage.

**Tell me what projects are going on now and how things have changed since leaving your community at Robert Taylor Homes?**
It's totally different. You can't ring a bell and a hundred children show up. It's hard to plan things. To get that particular group together, again, well, it will never be that occasion again.

So now we work with people to grow stuff in their backyards. We're just trying to do one family at a time instead of all of them at once. So that's the way we're approaching it. We touch about forty families every year in one way or another. We just encourage people to grow their own, to not be afraid of growing on their own, and to let the kids be involved so that they'll start eating right.

We have also had land in Dawson, Illinois, at the Karaal Farm donated to us to house our animals. We got some new ones, including goats that were gifted to us by the Angelic Organics Learning Center. Then we have crops in Union Pier, Michigan, at Hidden Haven, which is also generously donated and which we share with some other wonderful small farmers.

**How has this new urban/rural connection impacted the families you work with?**
It used to be that during the summertime you went down south to swim in a creek and do all those outdoor things. This generation has lost those land connections. Nobody can swim, and they're not eager to get in the water. It's a detriment that we've lost those connections to the wilderness, to nature. We're trying to change that. We take kids out to one of our rural farms on trips and retreats.

Once they're there one day, they always want to come back under any circumstance. I think that's an expansion we never even thought about while we were doing food or even making the gardens until we worked at a friend's farm in central Illinois and then interacted with the goats—it's just magnificent. It's a totally different thing. I think the livestock really brings a lot to the picture.

**You are also teaching after-school courses out of a greenhouse on the far south side of Chicago. What is your curriculum like?**
That space is also donated, by Scott Parker's Urban Farm South—through collaboration is really how we get things done. At the greenhouse, the kids come and learn to make their own soil. They have to start four different compost systems. We give them a worm bucket, they take it home, keep it a week, and bring it back. Sometimes it's disheartening when they come back with it empty because no one has eaten even one meal at home in seven days. That becomes an opportunity for us to talk about the connection between everyday eating and what we are doing with the soil. So then they actually start the compost. They see the cycle from the seed all the way to actually cooking with what they have produced.

**Where would you like to see God's Gang in five years?**
I'd really like to see us continuing what we do, just on a bigger scale. We need a city site that is not here at my house, that is more formal, that is more of a business. We really could just develop the 83rd Street site we already work with, those five greenhouses, that'd be enough.

On the other hand, I'm just in love with being in my neighborhood right here. I love that people can come in through the gate, get what they want, take it home, and plant it or eat it. I'm not asking anybody to fill out any papers. We're just communing. I hope to get all of our neighbors together to see what each one has done at the end of the season, sort of like you do garden walks but with a focus on food. Of course, I want to increase what we're doing at Hidden Haven and Karaal Farm. I want to be able to bring more kids out of the city and to these places.

Pages 162–163
Ezekiel Thomas and Michelle "Little Bird" Thomas are at God's Gang headquarters in Carolyn Thomas's backyard.

# Participation Park

Location:
**Baltimore, Maryland**

Organizing body:
**3 founding partners, plus occasional volunteers**

Scale:
**½ acre**

Type:
**Volunteer-Run**

Currently producing:
**Tomatoes, greens, peppers, and watermelon**

In operation:
**Since 2007**

Web site:
**baltimoredevelopmentco-op.org**

Three painting students who met in art school in Baltimore found themselves in a typical predicament—what does it mean to make two-dimensional portraits and representations when the world, and Baltimore in particular, is so richly complex, challenging, and contradictory? The path these artists chose was not a typical one, though. For several years they experimented in making art that blended with the life of the city: They led walking tours, hosted gatherings with local activists to learn more about neighborhood history, and they even designed and built a trailer for their car that could unfold into a stage for organizing protests or giving away free food or clothing to fellow residents. They connected with curators from a local art museum to work on exhibitions highlighting this approach to artistic practice, as well as with a local activist newspaper to spread and exchange ideas with others in their city and beyond. After several years of doing small-scale and temporary projects

around town, the three began to think seriously about longevity and putting roots down in Baltimore, a city that has long suffered from abandonment—something they did not want to perpetuate by leaving or disinvesting the way many postcollege students do with their adopted homes. Scott Berzofsky reflected, "We wanted to try to extend that experiment for a longer period of time. So instead of going to a street corner or a vacant lot and doing something for one day, we asked ourselves, 'What if we did something for a year, for two years?'" And so the group decided to poke around town looking for an abandoned building that they could occupy. The building would serve as the venue for all of the work they had been doing and wanted to develop—a community cultural center that directly opposed the accepted notion that landowners could build up, let fall down, or let sit derelict the inner-city housing stock while thousands of people live in the streets or without basic necessities.

Once they found a building they thought would work, they ended up focusing their attention on the massive series of vacant lots next to the building (Baltimore's landscape is characterized by unoccupied lots and structures). That is when Participation Park came into being.

# Interview with Nicholas Wisniewski, Scott Berzofsky, and Dane Nester

**What motivated you to start this work?**
**Nicholas Wisniewski, collective member**: For me, Participation Park wasn't really about urban agriculture in the beginning. It was about reclaiming vacant space, the commons, and working against the increasing privatization of public spaces and the top-down forms of urban planning that design them. Baltimore is plagued with ubiquitous abandonment: about forty thousand vacant houses and twelve thousand vacant lots. We wanted to collaborate with residents to address the absurdity of private property and speculative development that allows this kind of abandonment and blight to happen, and instead create a different kind of space from the bottom up that responds to collective needs and desires. And while thinking of different strategies for squatting that wouldn't result in immediate eviction, we decided to create a smoke screen out of the growing enthusiasm around "going green." But we were sincere about growing vegetables, too.

We began by using food as this sort of Trojan horse to avoid eviction while subverting private-property laws, because who would evict people growing organic vegetables that were being distributed for free? At the same time, we were revalorizing land-use possibilities in a place that had been abandoned and was riddled with dumping problems. We tried to build participation and a sense of collective reownership just through a modest day-to-day presence. Just being there every day, talking to people about different possibilities, we started to transform this abandoned lot into a vegetable garden.

**How does the local economy impact your work or how you work?**
**NW**: The extreme economic inequality that exists in the city directly reflects the extreme racial segregation in Baltimore. The poorest, most blighted sections of the city are majority African American—the process of ghettoization constricts city services, kills businesses, and empties out jobs.

Participation Park is located in this context, and so we have been interested in developing sustainable economic alternatives. We want to be more autonomous and independent of nonprofit grants. We decided to experiment with nonalienating labor opportunities that are worker-controlled and -owned, both for participants from the neighborhood and for us as well. And to shift our artist practice away from

Above:
Martin and Tony taking out
crabgrass.

this charity, self-sacrificing engagement with the "community" whereby you privilege someone else's struggle over your own, and instead proceed with socially
equitable projects of solidarity.

We are also trying to establish this worker-run cooperative for next season to
sustain our more experimental cultural practice.

### So how would the cooperative work?

**NW**: It will be based on cooperative principles such as mutual aid, fair wages,
and democratic decision-making processes. The cooperative Huerta del Centro/
Downtown Farm is just a hybridized part of the larger Participation Park working to
build self-organized infrastructures and counterinstitutions. The **co-op** will not only
be concerned with maintaining a healthy **co-op** for its workers but also preventing
gentrification in the neighborhood and increasing people's control over land and
collective forms of development.

**Scott Berzofsky, collective member**: We're doing the co-op in collaboration with Latino immigrants from southeast Baltimore.

**NW**: This year we're going to fence off half of the land to start this co-op, but we'll still have a large communal garden with no fence. The co-op will include a CSA, we'll have a farm stand at local markets, permitted or guerrilla, and sell to local restaurants. We'll be selling vegetables to other worker-run co-ops that share our principles as well as to high-end restaurants from whom we can charge more money—the idea being that we can generate enough surplus to both pay co-op members a fair wage and subsidize more experimental activities at Participation Park.

**A fence in Participation Park seems somewhat contradictory to your initial model. Did it take some time to realize the necessity in the face of income?**
**NW**: Yes, three years' worth. Negotiating public space is messy, constant, and wonderful, in many respects. From my experiences, if you want to start a commercial farm in the city as a livelihood and gamble your monthly paycheck, you have to have a fence. To sell products and vegetables you need security. And a fence alone will not do that—people need to see value in the product and how it will benefit the community.

**Dane Nester, collective member**: There's so much gleaning that occurs at Participation Park that it's obvious why the co-op participants would want a fence. People's paychecks are at stake, and the co-op needs to be tested as an economic alternative. If the co-op really works as an economic alternative, then we can figure out how to operate without a fence.

**NW**: We encourage gleaning, but we don't just want people to glean, we want them to help, because ideally it's a reciprocal thing. It's the only way it can be sustainable.

**SB**: We started out with some money from small foundation grants and donations. We also took advantage of other city resources, for example the Department of Parks and Recreation will give you free wood chips and leaf mulch. And we've been getting free water from the city from the fire hydrant—all the fire hydrants in the inner city have locks on them so you can't just open them, so we asked some firefighters to remove the lock and they were surprisingly helpful. We've gotten a nonprofit to come out and till for us with their Bobcat, and we're having some trees

Right, top:
(Standing, from left) Scott
Berzofsky, Miss Helen, and
Wisniewski; (kneeling) Kitt
Repass and Dane Nester.

Right, bottom:
Melissa Weinberg plants a
kids' garden with Johnston
Square neighborhood youth.

cut down this spring by the Forestry Division. So there are cool people working for the city and local nonprofits who have supported the project, who have the ability to redirect their resources if they want to.

**NW**: But we also had a letter from the University of Maryland Cooperative Extension saying we had permission to use the fire hydrant, which was based on us lying to them about having permission to use the land. All of the grants we received were based on this kind of white lie. We fabricated a web of fictions that reinforced each other in order to build legitimacy.

**SB**: For example, if people see the city trucks coming to dump wood chips, or we get a grant from a local foundation, or the former Governor William Donald Schaefer visits on a tour with the Baltimore Community Foundation, it all contributes to this illusion of legitimacy. We have this hilarious photo of us with Schaefer at the farm.

**NW**: We were bartering for a while, too. Also, there is this group, RICA (Regional Institute for Children and Adolescents), in west Baltimore that has a horticulture center. They have a greenhouse for growing plants and vegetables that would get thrown out each year if not given away, so we partnered with them.

**How could your work be coordinated with other initiatives at the policy or community level to restructure how systems work?**
**DN**: We're still trying to understand how to engage with other initiatives. This year we participated with many others in the Baltimore Urban Agriculture Task Force to create more jobs in urban agriculture and increase the acreage of farmable land in Baltimore.

**SB**: The whole project has sort of an antagonistic attitude—squatting and all. But it's not like we feel as if we're somehow outside the larger network of relationships that constitute the city. We're constantly in dialogue or partnering with people, nonprofit groups, city officials, community groups, and educational institutions. And this task force does have potential—they're already changing zoning regulations regarding livestock in the city.

**Baltimore Urban Agriculture Task Force**
A coalition of farmers, students, professionals, artists, parents, and concerned citizens whose mission is to produce food locally. Among several of its core goals is to have six hundred jobs in urban agriculture within four years. Another objective is to have ten acres of farmable land in the city of Baltimore in the next year, and one hundred acres by 2012.

Above:
Wisniewski and Michelle
Belfield pose with their first
heirloom tomato harvest.

Above, right:
Snacking on fresh greens,
straight from the soil to table.

Right:
Wisniewski harvests lettuce
surrounded by ad hoc rainwater containers made from
reclaimed highway barriers.

# Anarchy Apiaries

Location:
**Hudson Valley, New York**

Organizing body:
**1 founder**

Scale:
**30 locations throughout
the Hudson Valley**

Type:
**Artist run**

Currently producing:
**Bees**

In operation:
**Since 2007**

Web site:
**anarchyapiaries.org**

A project of twenty-eight-year-old Sam Comfort, Anarchy Apiaries is a one-man operation with the mission to raise treatment-free honeybees. He currently has three hundred hives spread out across fifteen farms in the Hudson Valley of New York state. The land is given to him in exchange for honey, but honey is not what Sam's work is about. His work is really about rebuilding the domestic honeybee through less-invasive and treatment-free hives. He uses a top-bar hive design, which counters the industry's Langstroth hive, which employs a premolded plastic comb.

In 2006, the world was shocked by the news of "Colony Collapse Disorder," a condition that describes the dramatic decline of the honeybee in North America. Comfort's theory is that the bee has been debilitated by this system, in that they don't have to work as hard, so they have become weak and susceptible to disease. He started the bee club Beekeepers Association of Northern Dutchess, which comprises serious beekeepers and hobbyists alike who meet monthly. The former art student's goal is to rebuild the DNA of the honeybee to strengthen it to resist disease and the varroa mite that plagues most of the United States' "domestic" honeybees.

Opposite, top:
Sam Comfort's bees create 100 percent of their own hive comb; they do not build off premolded wax. Sam swears this activity helps keep his bees healthy and docile.

Opposite, bottom:
The nodule on the edge of the comb indicates a queen is developing within.

# Interview with Sam Comfort

## Can you describe the context you are working in?

Dutchess County is close enough to harbor a culture of weekenders up from New York City, and young people had not been regularly putting roots down until the local-foods movement enabled their livelihood and access to land. It seems to me that up to this point in time, the price of living had stymied community in the Hudson Valley, about two hours' drive due north from New York City. Now many new, diverse organic farms and CSAs are sprouting, perhaps drawing energy down from Vermont, where a legacy of back-to-the-earth and homesteading has inspired generations to pursue alternative ways of living. Everything is just getting started here, and it is very exciting. We are inventing a new culture around our farms, finding nourishment in our camaraderie, and bringing the buzz to the Big City.

## How did you get into bees?

It was meant to *bee*. . . . I tell people I won six hives in a poker game, but that's not true, it's just the best thing I've come up with. I started at Bard College as a figurative painter. I found the **permaculture** bible by Bill Mollison at the library. It hadn't been checked out since the mid-'80s. The creativity in the bees' living structures is amazing! So I knew I wanted to go into agriculture, and bees became my way.

I contacted Todd Hardy at Honey Gardens in Vermont who said that I could park my van out by the honey house, camp out, and stay all summer and learn about bees. It was great. He has about a thousand hives producing raw honey.

That fall I got a job as a beekeeper in Montana. It was a five-thousand-hive operation on pallets, which you moved with a forklift. Everything was really industrial and streamlined, very by-the-book. It was very different from what I had been doing in Vermont. We did almond pollination in California, apples in Washington, cherries around Blackfoot Lake in Montana, and sweet clover honey crop, too.

The hives would be stacked four to six on a pallet, making five hundred hives on a semi with a giant net over them. You send 'em on down the road two thousand miles, shaking them the whole way.

**Bill Mollison**
Researcher, scientist, teacher, naturalist, and author of *Permaculture One: A Perennial Agriculture for Human Settlements*. He is considered to be the "father of permaculture," an integrated system of design, codeveloped with David Holmgren, that encompasses not only agriculture, horticulture, architecture, and ecology, but also economic systems, land-access strategies, and legal systems for businesses and communities.

Opposite:
Solar-powered beeswax-melting tray.

**Can you talk about the work you are focusing on?**
In order to keep bees alive, my business has three elements: genetics, being
treatment-free, and outreach. First, my queens have diverse genetics. The gene
pool has become too shallow in this country—it needs to be rebuilt. Second,
I establish bees that can survive without any treatments of antibiotics and without
artificial feedings, which means less-invasive beekeeping, having a natural cell
size within the hive, using methods that are less expensive for new beekeepers,
and doing less to manipulate the bees. The third thing I do is outreach—starting
the Dutchess County group, giving lectures.

On average, I'm younger than most beekeepers by twenty to thirty years. I am
not the youngest commercial beekeeper I know, but I am the youngest who's not
inheriting a business. I realized I had a role to play in the industry. I met people who
were dedicated to raising hives treatment-free, and they became my mentors. I've
had a lot of support thanks to the media and the public. The path just came to me.

**Is there a season for bees or is it year-round?**
At this point I am still "cheating" and bringing certain hives down to Florida for the
winter to keep those bees alive and change out their queen. Most of my bees will
make it here, so I only take the ones that won't survive. Once the bees get to
Florida they start making honey right away, whereas if they stayed up here they
would die. I'm trying to create stock that's hardy enough to survive New York winters.
Ideally I want to be a stationary beekeeper and have hives that will winter here.

**How do you get them to Florida?**
I drive with bees all the time up and down the East Coast in my little pickup and
trailer. You just don't stop—and it's a twenty-hour drive. When you get there you
have to unload the bees before first light, because you don't want them to be
under that net. It is the hardest thing I do all year.

**Is it true that in industrial beekeeping bees are fed corn syrup?**
Yeah, and soy flour for protein. In almond orchards, there would be fourteen hundred hives in one row. Four hives to a pallet. They use a gasoline nozzle–looking
thing hooked up to a truck with a three-hundred-gallon tank of corn syrup and fill
up the troughs. If they didn't do that, the bees would die. Some of these bees are
taking in twelve to thirteen gallons of corn syrup through the winter just to subsist,
just to be alive. They used to be divine creatures in every culture except ours, and
now they are just livestock.

Above, left:
One of the sites that hosts Sam Comfort's hives. He trades his landlords honey for use of the land, which he calls "rent honey."

Above, right:
No bees, no pollination, no blueberries.

**Why did you work in the industrial side of bees?**
I learned the ropes, I learned what not to do. I learned exactly how to kill bees.

**What about hobbyist beekeeping? Is there any support for this type of beekeeping?**
Hobbyist beekeepers, which are really the future, don't have an alternative to these industrial bees. The gene pool is so weak these days that it's hard to find bees that can survive on their own without going to artificial crutches.

North Carolina subsidizes new beekeepers. [But the program] is only for those who are starting from scratch. You don't get money, but they give you a kit with a plastic foundation and a whole line of chemicals to keep the bees alive. The bees are shipped up from Georgia. It's a neat idea, but it's not really helping anything.

**How is honey part of your project?**
It's a tough life trying to make a living selling honey. It's not a life I would wish on anybody. Most of the honey in this country comes from China or Argentina. A lot of the time it's not even really honey. Even U.S.-produced honey is laced with these miticides that keepers have been putting in since the '80s. They're organo-phosphates, nerve agents, really sketchy stuff. It's a huge cover-up by the National Honey Board. So in a way, corn syrup is really benign in comparison.

You just have to know your beekeeper, or anyone who's growing your food. I don't trust organic food. I like to know my farmers, how they grow, what's on their bookshelves, the whole deal.

Organic honey usually comes from Brazil or Chile, and those countries don't have an EPA equivalent. Certified honey in this country goes by the state, and most states will not touch it, because they generally require a three-mile radius around your hives without any spraying, which means no roads, no power lines, nobody spraying Roundup in their backyards either.

## What does "treatment-free" beekeeping mean?

What some of us are doing now is against the grain of commercial industries, even though it hasn't been that way for several generations. Modern beekeeping was begun in the 1850s by a minister in Philadelphia named Lorenzo Langstroth—thus modern, commercial boxes are called Langstroth hives. He took note of the bee space, which is a three-eighths-inch space between the combs, and if you maintain that space from comb to comb to comb, you can build these wooden frames so that you can pull them out and reorder them. Before that, bees were kept in steps, straw domes, or gums, which are hollowed-out logs. You never went into the beehive. You just let the bees swarm, and that is what they've done for millions of years.

With the new hives, you could simulate the swarm by pulling out extra bees, or brood, and rather than cutting out the wax and mashing it up, you could cut out the wax, spin it to remove the honey, and then give the wax back to the bees the next year for them to use again. Once they started doing that, all these pathogens appeared. The comb is like a filter, or the liver of the hive. It would soak up all the pesticides and pathogens causing these diseases. The main one was American Foulbrood, which began in the 1870s and 1880s. Once that happened, every state decided to ban fixed-comb beekeeping, and to this day it is still illegal. That helped to create this monopoly for profit. It locked everyone into this standardized shape and new method. You just had to throw bees into a box and they did great. Several generations followed.

If you go into any supply shop and say, "I don't know anything about bees, but I want to get started," they will give you what looks like a plastic coffin. It comes with a premade comb that is bigger than the bees would naturally make on their own. Since the bees don't have to work as hard, it's like taking away their will to live.

I keep some bees in what's called a top-bar hive, but I also keep Langstroth's. With top-bar hives, these bees are drawing wax. They secrete the wax from their abdomens and they lick it off each other and then mold it into combs. They use their bodies as measurements. So, smaller bees will make smaller-size cells. It takes several generations to get to a standard cell size.

## Venom Therapy

Bee venom therapy, also known as *apitherapy*, utilizes bee venom in the treatment of many health conditions including arthritis, rheumatism, back pain, skin diseases, Lyme disease, and chronic fatigue syndrome. Bee venom comes from the stingers of honeybees. It is a rich source of enzymes, peptides, and biogenic amines. There are at least eighteen active components in the venom that have some pharmaceutical properties.

Traditionally, bee venom was administered with live bees by stimulating them to sting in the affected area, trigger points, or acupuncture points. Depending on the nature of the disease, the standardized venom can be used in a cream, liniment, ointment, or injection form.

### Are you seeing more interest in bees?

It used to be that the only question I ever got asked was whether I got stung. But now people ask, "What's going on with the bees? How can we help you with the bees?" or say, "We hear they aren't doin' so well."

Honeybees are our only connection to the insect world. They are so beneficial in everything they do. Bees are a gateway bug for people to realize that everything has its place. We need to think of our ecosystems as everything that is living there. We need wild areas that support our native pollinators and everything else that goes on; we don't need to control everything and plow it over and plant in rows. The bees are going to be just fine. We need to let them do their thing and stop artificially supporting them. It's the people who need the help. Bees are just the vehicle.

### How many times have you been stung in your life?

A lot. It's in the thousands. I have had several-hundred-sting days. After a couple dozen stings, they stop hurting. When I first started there were months when I couldn't close my hands because they were too swollen, and I'd have my eyes swollen shut for three days.

I hardly get stung these days. I start to miss it if I haven't been stung in a while. You sleep better at night after getting stung. Bee sting therapy predates Chinese acupuncture. Beekeepers are known for very low cancer rates and longevity.

### How did you connect with the people who are hosting your bees on their land?

I responded to an ad about two years ago. They wanted someone to keep bees on their land in exchange for honey. I give these folks twenty to thirty pounds of rent honey, which they like in the wax.

### And do people get anything else for hosting your bees?

Recently, the New York state agricultural tax exemption laws were changed. Formerly to qualify for ag exemption you had to make $10,000 per plot of land. Now as a beekeeper I just have to make ten grand and all my landowners can get ag exemption. So even though no farming is being done on this land, the owners can qualify for property tax ag exemption.

**How does the local economy affect you? And why are you here specifically?**
I chose this land because of its proximity to New York City, because I have a lot of resources here. I went to college nearby, and I still have friends here. I was getting tired of industrial beekeeping in Montana, even though I loved it there, so when I wanted to start my own beekeeping I wanted to be here.

**Is there a policy or regulation that would help your mission?**
To be the most vocal about bees I wanted to be close to the biggest think tank in the world. That's why I started here, close to New York City. There's a big movement to legalize beekeeping in NYC. It has been illegal for the past thirty years or so. You would figure that bees are a wild animal and stuff, but recent polls claim that there are at least eighteen hundred beekeepers within city limits. I know a bunch.

I've gotten bees in Chinatown. The ones I saw looked healthy and had a lot of pollen already. But, in the long term, I don't know about the sustainability of keeping bees in the city. At the same time, though, people put in all these flowering plants, and once they bloom they just rip them up and put in new flowering plants. There's some serious basswood trees lining the streets in Manhattan, too, which are a good honey flow. You can smell them at the start of June. The air gets thick with nectar. Once they do decide to legalize it, I'd take my bees down to the botanical garden.

In terms of policy, I would like to see more protected areas that are allowed to go wild. I think wildness is the salvation of the planet.

**Do you like those bees at the White House?**
Yeah, I haven't seen them, but you know, beekeeping is illegal in Washington, D.C.

**How could your work be coordinated with other initiatives?**
On a community level I am trying to get bees everywhere, on each farm and in backyards, on rooftops. Once you get tied to keeping bees you look more at the flowering plants and health of the soil, and you start to realize what needs changing in your environment. You become more aware.

Getting people involved with bees is about getting rid of fear, and having people overcome their fear overturns our whole social system. Our society runs on fear and greed and money—these drive our economic system. To go against that is really revolutionary.

Right:
Bee happy.

### Bee Basics

#### Brood

The term *brood* is used to refer to the embryo or egg, the larva, and the pupa stages in the life of holometabolous insects. The brood of honeybees develops within a beehive. In man-made, removable-frame hives, such as Langstroth hives, each frame that mainly consists of brood is called a *brood frame*. Brood frames usually have some pollen and nectar or honey in the upper corners of the frame. The rest of the brood frame cells may be empty or occupied by brood in various developmental stages. During the brood-raising season, the bees may reuse the cells from which brood have emerged for additional brood or convert them to honey or pollen storage. Bees show remarkable flexibility in adapting cells to a use best suited for the hive's survival.

#### Drones

*Drones* are male honeybees. Drones develop from eggs that have not been fertilized.

#### Worker Bee

A *worker bee* is any female bee that lacks the full reproductive capacity of the colony's queen bee. Honeybee workers keep the hive temperature uniform in the critical brood area. Workers gather pollen into the pollen baskets on their back legs and then carry it back to the hive, where it is used as food for the developing brood. Pollen carried on their bodies may be transported to another flower, where a small portion can rub off onto the pistil, resulting in cross-pollination.

#### Queen Bee

The *queen bee* is an adult, mated female developed from larvae selected by worker bees and specially fed in order to become sexually mature. There is normally only one adult, mated queen in a hive.

#### How the Hive Works

Bee brood frames comprise brood at various stages of development: eggs, larvae, and pupae. In each cell of honeycomb, the queen lays an egg, gluing it to the bottom of the cell. As the egg hatches, worker bees add royal jelly—a secretion from glands on the heads of young bees. For three days the young larvae are fed royal jelly, then they are fed nectar or diluted honey and pollen. A few female larvae in special queen cups may be selected to become queens. Their special queen cups are flooded with royal jelly for six days. The extra royal jelly speeds up the queen larvae development. Only the queen will have fully developed ovaries, meaning she will be sexually mature. Drone brood develops from unfertilized eggs. Drone brood cells are larger than the cells of female worker bees.

# Afterword

### The Questions That Need To Be Asked Now

We hope that you learn as much from this book as we learned from these inspiring people. By presenting them in all of their diversity and complexity together, we hope to say that none of those banners for a new food system can move forward if this assortment of people and the far-reaching subcultures and tendencies they represent are not in it together somehow.

The challenges that we face are not new but are simply new variations on themes we have long encountered. So we must not look back fifty years or five hundred years or five thousand with some nostalgia for things past. From the beginning of European colonization, this land—and many of its people—has been beaten down and mistreated for the exporting of resources. Sometimes for export to colonial powers, then to other regions of the country, then to regions that we sought to dominate in one way or another. But this dynamic has always been dominant: to grow food for exporting. A really strong local food system is not something we have really known in this country, beyond some of the practices of the Native American tribes or the settlers who emphasized subsistence farming over frontier expansion.

We need to grow a strong local food system to lessen our reliance on fossil fuels for production, processing, and transport. We need to alter our reliance on water for production, processing, and transport. This will require locally relevant and sensitive responses, as there are diverse places, climates, and resource distribution across this land. Technological "fixes," population density and the urban/rural divide, and unity of vision are the three key challenges and questions we observed in our travels, which we all need to work on together.

All of our past and present problems won't get a technological fix. Workers and especially farmer movements throughout the history of this land have had a difficult relationship to technology because it was used to make their labor obsolete. People with an eye and a heart for environmental agendas know that many of the technological fixes have had negative long-term health impacts on animals, people, and land. Throughout our interviews, conflicting views on technology appeared again and again from the people out there doing the work. And so it is not without critical hesitation that we should look toward technology. We need to take seriously the task of looking at energy-efficient technologies available at this historically unique moment that can facilitate year-round food production in different climates.

Another feature of our present moment is the difference in density of people in cities versus rural areas. According to the 2000 census, more than 80 percent of people in the United States live in broadly defined metropolitan areas. This presents challenges and opportunities. Some of the farmers suggested their scale was just too small to be more than symbolic, while others suggested it is everyone's job to subsist and to grow—for even just part of their food needs. Some of the farmers we spoke with felt very strongly that people needed to leave cities and return to the land while others offered hesitation at people jumping into new lives and work with which they might simply be incompatible. Can the density of urban areas be planned (or re-planned) in such a way that a combination of urban food growing and nearby rural growing can give people access to many different kinds of wonderful food to sustain life in all of the currently populated regions year-round?

And finally, there is the question of unity. The land, the work, and the vision that we explored and encountered in these twenty places had some incredible overlap and some remarkable dissonance. That wasn't surprising—after all, we picked these twenty examples because they were so different from one another. Farmers' movements during the past two centuries have all had trouble working past their differences and the diversity of people with which they should be in solidarity. The explosive growth of "vertically integrated" agribusiness corporations has produced a huge rift in scale (of both economy and culture) between big and small farms. Those same companies' encroachment into the expensive organics market, which is already seen as light on economic justice for poor workers and poor consumers, is further increasing divides between haves and have-nots. What is it going to take for the people who are doing the work of growing food and the people who are eating it to find some unity of vision?

These questions are places to proceed from. Ask them of your friends, local farmers, or backyard gardeners. Please keep the questions going; find people with good answers, and keep moving together.

P.S. And follow up with us at farmtogethernow.org.

# Glossary

### Adaptogenic
Herbs that are nontoxic and help to increase the body's resistance to stress, trauma, anxiety, and fatigue. They are considered to have a normalizing impact on the body's homeostasis, assisting with either toning down or strengthening imbalances.

### Agrobiodiversity
Also referred to as "agricultural diversity," agrobiodiversity is the result of the interaction among the environment, genetic resources and management systems, and practices used by culturally diverse peoples, resulting in land and water resources being used for production in different ways. Local knowledge and culture are considered integral parts of agrobiodiversity, because it is the human activity of agriculture that shapes and conserves this biodiversity.

### AmeriCorps
A federally funded community-service program initiated under President Bill Clinton in 1994. More than 500,000 people have worked in community organizations through its national and state programs, VISTA (Volunteers in Service to America), and NCCC (National Civilian Community Corps) projects.

### Bioclimatology
This interdisciplinary field of science explores the relationship between the biological makeup of Earth and the climate. The balance of life on Earth can have a huge impact on the climate and the seasons, while Earth's atmosphere can and has dramatically shaped how plant and animal life has developed.

### Biodynamic, fukuoka, and permaculture
There are many philosophies that inform approaches to what can generally be called "sustainable agriculture" or "ecological agriculture." Some of the most prominent include the practice of "biodynamics," which treats the farm as an organism in and of itself and emphasizes the use of manure and compost as a way of caring for the soil to limit the need for external inputs. In Japan, a method of farming without tilling or plowing the soil was promoted by Masanobu Fukuoka (author of *The One-Straw Revolution*). This method of "natural farming" is achievable without machines and has been called "do-nothing farming" because of its emphasis on farming consistently with the reproduction cycles in nature. One other philosophy is a "permaculture," deriving from the terms *permanent agriculture* as well as *permanent culture*, which also emphasizes an approach to farming that mimics nature. In this tradition, special attention is given to perennial plants that do not need to be replanted every season and to designing habitats and spaces for humans that are attentive to how we relate to other animals and natural systems.

### Biointensive method
Agricultural system that focuses on maximum yields from the minimum area of land, while simultaneously improving the soil. The goal of the method is long-term sustainability on a closed-system basis.

### Bioregion
Also known as an "ecoregion," a bioregion refers to a naturally defined area featuring distinct watershed boundaries, soil type, vegetation, climate, and terrain and/or aquatic characteristics. The philosophy of bioregionalism extends this thinking to the cultural and political realm by encouraging the need for solutions that build on local knowledge, which is not bound to arbitrarily defined political territory.

### Biotechnology
Broadly understood, this term applies to any kind of process or product that is derived from living organisms or biological processes. Specifically in relation to the industry of agriculture, it is the catchall for any kind of manipulation of life through science for a commercial use. The criticisms relating to biotechnology relate closely to the terms *genetically modified organisms* and *Monsanto*, both of which are defined in this glossary, in that they focus on the ethics and health implications associated with patenting and manipulating naturally occurring life processes.

### CAFO
Concentrated (or Confined) Animal Feeding Operations are features consistently found in agricultural settings known as "factory farms." These lots hold animals close together with little mobility and can be indoor or outdoor. According to the Environmental Protection Agency (EPA), CAFOs can confine animals for up to forty-five days in a twelve-month period and do not supply grass or other vegetation during the normal growing season*.

There are many reports of CAFO confinement lasting much longer, and the absence of grass in the lot indicates the connection between this approach to raising animals for meat and the dramatic transition to feeding cows, pigs, and other animals corn and soy in place of the vegetation they would naturally eat. CAFOs are at the center of many food debates, including their role in food safety, environmental problems caused by their waste, stench and runoff water, and animal rights.
*This definition specifically relates to AFOs, of which CAFOs are a subset.

### Collective farm
A collective farm shares power among member-owners, who make decisions on a consensus-driven and egalitarian basis. Collectives differ from cooperatives in that they are not necessarily focused upon an economic benefit.

### Co-op

There are many approaches to organizing agricultural cooperatives that allow resources to be pooled among a group of farmers. The less common are production cooperatives, whereby the production process is actually done by farmers working together. The more common cooperative is a "service cooperative," which exists when farmers share the responsibility for supply (purchasing things they need to run the farm in large quantities and splitting them up) or in marketing (working together on pricing, processing, packaging, and distribution of their shared products).

### CSA

Community Supported Agriculture is a way for individuals to pledge support to a local farm. An individual or family becomes a shareholder by buying "shares" in the farm through an advance pledge that covers anticipated costs of the farm operation and farmers' salaries. In return, shareholders receive a box of seasonal vegetables each week throughout the farming season. This arrangement creates a shared risk such that if a flood were to impact a certain crop, the consumers and the farm would both feel the impact.

### Demonstration project

A project designed to illustrate the potential of a larger initiative, often with hopes of testing methods and approaches that may be expensive or impractical to implement without proof of the need for such services first.

### Direct action

Often defined as a political or social response to a challenge that involves directly addressing a problem by the people who have been directly impacted, as opposed to going through representational or legislative channels to make demands. Often the means are confrontational, such as strikes, sit-ins, and squatting.

### Environmental Protection Agency (EPA)

Created in 1970 by President Nixon, the Environmental Protection Agency is responsible for enforcing policy related to the health of humans and the environment. The agency is responsible for well-known legislative acts relating to endangered species, scenic landscapes, fuel-economy of automobiles, and clean air and water. The EPA has been criticized for not doing enough to curb greenhouse gas emissions or regulate the automobile industry in accordance with their Clean Air Act.

### Farmers' market coupon program

There is a recognition in many places that healthful food is out of reach for many residents living on low or fixed incomes. Through a variety of approaches, the organizers of farmers' markets, as well as local, state, and federal agencies responsible for food and welfare, have provided access to farm-fresh foods with the creation of subsidized coupons for use at markets. These coupons make access to food a reality for many who otherwise could not afford it, while also connecting farmers to new and often more-diverse customer bases to support their work.

### Federation of Southern Cooperatives

Formed in 1967 as a direct outgrowth of the civil rights movement, the FSC works to encourage black farmers' cooperatives and land retention. At one point, the FSC coordinated the activities of 130 co-ops across the South; today it works with 35 cooperatives representing 12,000 black family farms. Its Rural Training and Research Center in Epes, Alabama, trains people to start co-ops in farm management and in the creation of credit unions for cooperative management of capital. As an organization, it was instrumental in fighting for the fair treatment of African American farmers by the U.S. government, including such prominent cases as Pigford v. Glickman, which resulted in a class-action settlement in 1999. The case argued that thousands of African American farmers were discriminated against by the Department of Agriculture's credit, benefit, and subsidy programs. In 1985 the FSC merged with the Land Assistance Fund and began to focus an increasing amount of energy on black landownership.

Since the destruction resulting from Hurricane Katrina in 2005, the FSC has facilitated trainings on cooperative development for farmers affected by the storm and has served as a distributor of resources from food to fuel to equipment donated by other co-ops across the country through its alliance with the National Family Farm Coalition. See Federation.coop for more information.

### Food First

Also known as the Institute for Food and Development Policy, Food First is a nonprofit organization based in Oakland, California, whose mission is to eliminate the injustices that cause hunger. Founded in 1975 by Frances Moore Lappé, author of *Diet for a Small Planet*, it is a think tank and "education-for-action center."

### Food justice

A loose-knit social movement focusing on the belief that global hunger is not the result of a lack of food but the lack of political will to ensure its fair distribution, regardless of peoples' ability to pay for it. Sometimes called a "human right to food," the term is used to unite and describe food-centered activism that connects to traditions of economic, environmental, and social justice. At the center of this emerging discourse and movement is the concept of self-reliance and self-determination for all people to determine their own solutions to their food needs.

### Fukuokas

*See* Biodynamic.

## Gleaning

The act of collecting leftover crops from farmers' fields after they have been commercially harvested or from fields where it is not economically profitable to harvest. Some ancient cultures promoted gleaning as an early form of a welfare system. For example, ancient Jewish communities required that farmers not reap all the way to the edges of a field so as to leave some for the poor and for strangers.

## GMOs

Simply put, genetically modified organisms are the resulting product of new genetic material being added to an organism's genome. This takes place commonly in many different sectors of science, with applications ranging from medicine to agriculture. The debates around GMOs, and more specifically on genetic engineering (GE) in food production, focus on the potential for the technology to introduce new allergens into the food chain and on the ethical concerns of modifying or controlling life processes without the ability to assess the long-term implications. At the center of the controversy is the ability of companies that are engineering genetics to patent the technology and therefore to have ownership over life.

## Grain-finished

The final months of an animal's life are important for the development of omega-3s and other nutrients, and so a diet consisting of a combination of grass and grains is ideal. Many farmers raise cattle in this manner, but those nutrients decrease dramatically if the animal is fattened using only grain feeding. There are not clear laws explaining what constitutes grass-fed beef, and therefore many meat-processing companies will package grain-finished beef with grass-fed labels.

## Heifer Project International

A nonprofit charitable organization founded by American farmer Dan West. It began as an organization dedicated to providing permanent freedom from hunger by giving families livestock and training so that they "could be spared the indignity of depending on others to feed their children." Its basic philosophy is based on the proverb "Give a man a fish; you have fed him for today. Teach a man to fish; you have fed him for a lifetime." Each participating family studies animal husbandry and agrees to donate any female offspring to another family. West imagined that a single gift would multiply far beyond the original investment. Nuestras Raíces (See page 110) has stretched Heifer's model of "passing on the gift" by distributing beginning loans instead of just the animals.

## Heritage grain

The southern Fertile Crescent is the ancient center of origin for wild wheat, the mother of all cultivated wheats. Wild wheat still grows in undisturbed meadows and field edges. Indigenous Fertile Crescent wheats have been selected by generations of traditional farmers and have richer flavor and more complex disease resistances than the modern wheat bred for yield and uniformity. An example of heritage grain is emmer, the wheat of ancient Egypt, found in the Jericho cave where Bar Kokhba rebels hid from the Romans in 135 CE.

## La Via Campesina

Formed in 1993, this network of 148 member organizations from 68 countries is an "international movement that coordinates peasant organizations of small- and middle-scale producers, agricultural workers, rural women, and indigenous communities from Asia, Africa, America, and Europe." The solidarity network is credited with popularizing the term "food sovereignty" as an alternative to the government-centered and often militarily enforced concept of food security.

## Marketing Agency in Common

A MAC is a unique form of cooperative organization that uses a federated structure to coordinate member organizations—a cooperative of cooperatives. It was instituted in 1922 with the passing of the Capper-Volstead Act, which set the ground rules for agricultural cooperatives in the United States. The assets of a MAC are owned by individual members as opposed to the MAC itself, giving it a more decentralized structure than most cooperatives, which can be useful if members want to maintain their own identities and structures yet still benefit from economies of scale.

## Monsanto

This transnational corporation based in St. Louis, Missouri, is focused on agricultural bio-technology. Its most popular product is an herbicide known as Roundup and an accompanying brand of soybean (and corn) known as Roundup Ready, which has been genetically engineered to resist the herbicide. In 2005, it finalized purchase of Seminis Inc., making it the world's largest conventional seed company. The corporation has been targeted continually by international activists who have ethical and economic critiques of its practice of patenting life through aggressive control of its seed products in intellectual property legal disputes.

## National Family Farm Coalition (NFFC)

A coalition of twenty-four grassroots farmer-led organizations spread throughout the United States founded during the credit crisis in 1986. These groups range from the American Raw Milk Producers and Family Farm Defenders to the Federation of Southern Cooperatives and the Community Farm Alliance in Kentucky. Their activities vary from advocating for their member organizations in Washington, D.C., to getting family farms prioritized over corporate agriculture in food policy to doing solidarity work with the international La Via Campesina network.

**Natural Resorces Conservation Service (NRCS)**

The Natural Resources Conservation Service (NRCS) is a federal organization originally founded by Congress in 1935 as the Soil Conservation Service (SCS). NRCS works closely with private landowners to assist in planning and conservation of soil, water, air, plants, and animals. The organization collaborates with USDA Service Centers to work on a local level in most counties in the United States.

**Permaculture**

See Biodynamics.

**Terra Madre and Slow Food**

Terra Madre is a network of food communities, each committed to producing quality food in a responsible, sustainable way. Terra Madre also refers to a major biannual conference held in Torino, Italy, intended to foster discussion and introduce innovative concepts in the fields of food, gastronomy, globalization, and economics. Terra Madre is coordinated by the Slow Food organization. Slow Food began in Italy with the 1986 foundation of its forerunner organization, Arcigola, to resist the opening of a McDonald's near the Spanish Steps in Rome. It was the first established part of the broader Slow movement that has since expanded globally to more than 100,000 members in 132 countries.

They consider themselves coproducers, not consumers, because they are informed about how their food is produced and actively support those who produce it, thus becoming a partner in the production process.

**United States Department of Agriculture (USDA)**

The USDA is the federal office responsible for administering policy on farming, agriculture, and food. Originally the department was a division of the Patent Office and then later a division of the Department of the Interior, until President Lincoln created the USDA in 1862. In 1889 President Cleveland elevated the department to a Cabinet level position. Since 1965, the department has issued most of its legislative priorities in a document casually referred to as a the Farm Bill. The USDA has an immense amount of power in areas ranging from the international trade and aid to nutrition and land use.

**Value-added product**

The difference between the raw material and the labor it takes to transform the raw material into something people will buy is the process of adding value. In agricultural work, this often takes the form of processing farm-raised plants and animals into specialty products that people will not only use more readily but that they'll often pay more for.

# Acknowledgments

Our people: Lauren Cumbia and Stijn Schiffeleers, and our families.

All of the farmers interviewed in the book; Anne Hamersky for showing these places and people in all their beauty, and for making the intense cross-country trek with such enthusiasm and positivity; Amy Treadwell, Jodi Warshaw, Doug Ogan, Andrew Schapiro, Michelle Clair, Peter Perez, and David Hawk; everyone from Chronicle Books; Brian Scott, our designer; Corinne Matesich for her amazing eye, hand, and imagination in the illustrations; Carla Avitabile, Alex Harker, and Ashley Weger for their transcription and research work; Mark Bittman for his openness and contribution to this effort; Courtney Moran, our enthusiastic blogging partner; Kelly Burdick gets a special callout for being so helpful in all things publishing and editing related; Adriane Colburn, Alex Harker, Michael Swaine, and Jonathan Meuser for their help in locating and visiting farms; Kyle Harris, Chris Carlsson and Adriana Camarena, and Aaron Sarver and Lisa Sousa for their hospitality during travels; for reading, editing, and feedback: Henrik Lebuhn, Lauren Cumbia, Todd Tucker, and Brian Holmes; for their responses to the initial project proposal: Nicolas Lampert, Heather Rogers, Dara Greenwald, Eric Triantafillou, Mark Shiply, Martha Boyd, Aaron Sarver, Annie Knepler, James Tracy, Kelly Burdick, David Meyers, Ryan Hollon, Rebecca Zorach, and Robin Schirmer; to Kathy and Lisa at National Family Farm Coalition; to friends and collaborators who are our regular go-to people for discussion and critique: Emily Forman, Micah Maidenberg, Josh MacPhee, Dara Greenwald, Brian Holmes, Claire Pentecost, Severine von Tscharner Fleming, all of the

AREA Chicago collaborators, and all of the Future-farmers collaborators; Sabrina Merlo for moral support; Justin Goh for camera help; Jason Reblando for advice on photography; and Bonnie Cecil for being a great farmer-activist from Kentucky.

In preparing for this book we talked, and we read, and we discussed. There is a wealth of writing about food and farms on bookshelves today that can help you make sense of what is on your plate and the world outside of your plate. Knowing what scholars and journalists in the field were saying helped us to prepare to learn what farmers and activists in the fields were saying. So thanks to these folks and ideas:

Wendell Berry says turn back the clock to simpler times; Wes Jackson says become native to your place; Michael Pollan says we need a food bill not a farm bill; Vandana Shiva says pay attention to the impact of biotechnology on farmers in developing countries; Mark Bittman says food matters; Sandor Katz shows us the margins of the food underground; José Bové gives us an example of farmer struggles in the age of global capitalism; Laura Lawson shows us how people grow food in the city and how sometimes projects fail; Raj Patel, Frances Moore Lappé, and Christopher Cook show us how people go hungry in the twenty-first century; Eric Schlosser details how we live in a fast-food nation; Carlo Petrini and Alice Waters want a slow-food world; John Zerzan thinks agriculture is the foundation of exploitation of humans and the land; Barbara Kingsolver tells us about food and family; Van Jones tells us that the green economy actually needs to include everyone; and the list goes on. We are indebted to them for their ideas and words.

# Biographies

### Amy Franceschini

Amy Franceschini is an artist and designer living in San Francisco, California. An overarching theme in her work is a perceived conflict between humans and nature. She creates work in various media that provides platforms to question this divide. Drawing inspiration from the improvisation, innovation, and collaboration that emerges from the choreographed activities of farming both big and small, her work often provides a playful entry point and tools for an audience to gain insight into a deeper field of inquiry—not only to imagine, but to participate in and initiate change in the places we live. In 1995, Franceschini founded Futurefarmers, an international collective of artists and designers that come together to make work that is relevant to the time and space surrounding them. Franceschini is a professor of Art + Architecture at the University of San Francisco and a visiting faculty in the graduate program at the California College of the Arts. You can visit her at futurefarmers.com.

### Daniel Tucker

Daniel Tucker works as an organizer and documentary maker with a focus primarily on places and the cultural and social movements that define them. From 2005 to 2010 he edited the biannual journal and discussion series *AREA Chicago*, releasing ten readers on themes related to culture and politics in Chicago. His conferences, classes, exhibitions, protests, writings, and lectures about the intersections of culture and politics have been seen throughout the United States and Europe. When not working on projects, he roasts fair-trade coffee on a grill in his alley and lives and eats in the northwest side of Chicago, Illinois, with his companion, Lauren. You can visit him at miscprojects.com.

### Mark Bittman

Mark Bittman is the author of *How to Cook Everything* and *Food Matters*, and of the weekly *New York Times* column, "The Minimalist." His work appeared in countless newspapers and magazines, and he is a regular on the *Today* show. Visit him at markbittman.com.

### Anne Hamersky

Anne Hamersky is a photographer who has focused on stories about agriculture for more than ten years. She has published her work in numerous magazines including *Time*, *LIFE*, *Yoga Journal*, and *Sierra*. She has exhibited at the Soros Foundation, the Civil Rights Institute, and the Oakland Museum. Her other books include *Expectations* (also from Chronicle Books), *Foods to Live By*, and *Inside Catholicism*. Born and raised in Nebraska, Anne lives in San Francisco, California, with her husband and their son, Joey, who rode shotgun during this cross-country odyssey. When she is not chasing the light, Anne swims in the open waters of the San Francisco Bay without a wet suit. See more of her work at annehamersky.com.

The authors are donating 50 percent of their profits from this book to a fund for new documentaries about food production in the United States. Find out more at farmtogethernow.org.

# Index